The SHE magazine
NAMES FOR BABY BOOK

The **SHE** magazine

NAMES FOR BABY BOOK

Catriona Luke

Michael O'Mara Books Limited

First published in 1995 by
Michael O'Mara Books Limited
9 Lion Yard
Tremadoc Road
London SW4 7NQ

1 3 5 7 9 10 8 6 4 2

A CIP catalogue record for this book is available from the
British Library

ISBN 1-85479-752-2

Designed and typeset by Florencetype Ltd, Stoodleigh, Devon
Printed and bound in England by Cox & Wyman, Reading

For the Six:
Anna, Giles, Alex, Francesca, Frances and Jesse,
and for Eliza Brown and
Kathryn Gooding

Warm thanks are due to
Diana Matthewman, Louis Jebe and Xa Younger
for introducing me to the wilder shores of Christian
names, and especially to James Fergusson,
who did all this and managed a generous canter through
the manuscript from A–Z.
Emmanuelle de la Lubie, Diana Pepper,
Helga Haack and Grania Fitzgerald gave both time
and advice, and the staff of two great institutions, the
British Library and the Register General of Scotland,
who smoothed the path of research and
collation of statistics.

Contents

A

Aaron (B)
Egyptian and Hebrew, meaning 'high mountain'. Aaron was the brother of Moses. An Old Testament name, it has recently entered the top 30 and looks set to become a name of the 90s.

Abel (B)
Hebrew, meaning 'breath'. In the Old Testament Abel was the second son of Eve and the brother of Cain.

Abigail (G)
Hebrew, meaning 'a father's joy'. It was a favourite of the Puritans on account of the description of an Abigail in the Book of Samuel as a woman of 'good understanding and of beautiful countenance'. Out of fashion in the 19th century, it has been revived in the second half of the present century.

Abraham (B)
Hebrew, meaning 'father of the multitude', the name given to Abram who became Father of the Israelites and was subsequently known as 'Abraham'. Always popular in the United States, it has the charming short form, Bram.

Ada (G)
Short form of Adelaide, meaning 'noble', which was popular in the 19th century.

Adah (G)
Hebrew, meaning 'ornament', and the first female name mentioned in the Book of Genesis.

Adair (B)
Celtic, meaning 'oak ford'.

Adam (B)
From Hebrew, meaning 'red earth'. According to the Book of Genesis Adam was the first man, literally made out of

the 'red earth'. It was a very popular name in the Middle Ages – one in three boys being called Adam – and was associated in the north of England with a Robin Hood-type character called Adam Bell and in Scotland with an Edom O'Gordon. Adam is now in the top ten list for boys.

Adamina (G)
Scottish feminine version of Adam which dates from the 18th century.

Adamnan (B)
Irish diminutive of Adam and the name of an eighth-century saint.

Adela (G)
From Old German, meaning 'noble', Adela was first adopted by the Normans as a royal name (William the Conqueror's daughter was called Adela) and was revived in the 19th century when there was a fashion for aristocratic Germanic names.

Adelaide (G)
French form of German Adelheid, meaning 'noble kind'. It was very popular in the early 19th century due to Queen Adelaide, the consort of William IV.

Adele (G)
Modern French form of the Old German Adela and a classic French name.

Adeline (G)
Old German, meaning 'nobility'. A popular medieval name, it came back into fashion in the 19th century.

Adina (G)
Hebrew, meaning 'voluptuous'.

Adrian (B)
Latin meaning 'of Adria', a seaport which gave its name to the Adriatic coast in Italy. Arrived in England in the seventh century after a saint and popular for a millennium. In this century it has been revived.

Adriana (G)
Feminine form of Adrian used by Shakespeare in *The Comedy of Errors*.

Adrienne (G)
French feminine form of Adrian which has been in English usage since the 50s.

Aeneas (B)
Greek, meaning 'one who is proud' and the name of the Trojan hero. It was popular in Italy in the 16th century and, surprisingly, for a number of centuries in Scotland and Ireland where it was used as an anglicization of Aonghus or Angus.

Agatha (G)
From Greek, meaning 'good' and the name of a third-century Sicilian saint. It was revived in the 19th century when there was a fashion for classical Greek and Roman names.

Agnes (G)
From Greek, meaning 'pure'. Along with Elizabeth and Joan it was one of the commonest girls' names in the Middle Ages, pronounced Ann-ese in the French fashion. When it was revived in the 19th century it was with the harsher pronunciation of Agg-ness which found favour in the fashion for Germanic-sounding names.

Agneta (G)
Latin form of Agnes, meaning 'pure', popular in northern Europe, particularly Scandinavia.

Aidan (B)
Charming Old Celtic name, meaning 'fire' or 'inspiration'. The seventh-century saint of Lindisfarne was so called. The name was revived for its historical and religious associations in the 19th century, also with the spelling Aden.

Aileen (G)
English spelling of the Irish Eibhlín, pronounced Eye-leen or Ev-leen.

Ailsa (G)
Scottish, from Old Gaelic 'al' or 'aill' meaning 'a rock'. Ailsa Craig is a rocky outcrop in the Firth of Clyde.

Heroic names

Late-18th-century parents were fond of giving their children names which might inspire them to great deeds, such as Lysander, Hercules, Hector, Ulysses or Alexander, or to particular religious devotion, such as Calvin, Luther or Wesley. In two cases it worked: Horatio Nelson (Horatio after the Roman hero who held the bridge across the Tiber against the Etruscans) and Arthur Wellesley (Arthur after the ancient English king) both lived up to the promise of their namesakes, becoming Admiral Lord Nelson and Duke of Wellington, respectively. Soon there was a new fashion for naming children after living heroes, and as the British Empire expanded there was a whole host to choose from. The fame of Admiral Rodney, Clive of India and General Gordon of Khartoum brought new names into circulation. Battle names were not exempt: Nelson's triumph at Cape St Vincent (1797) produced a revival of Vincent, a victory at Alma in the Crimea in 1854 resulted in a flurry of girls bearing the name. Stanley became popular in the 1870s following the meeting of the Welsh journalist Henry Morton Stanley with David Livingstone at Ujiji on Lake Tanganyika in 1871. The Boer War and the Zulu War produced Baden (after Robert Baden-Powell) and Redvers (after the British general Redvers Henry Buller who won a VC for his defence of Hlobane in 1879).

Happily the Victorians loved heroines as well: Grace, after Grace Darling who became a national heroine in 1838 when she rowed through storm conditions to rescue the survivors of the steamboat *Forfarshire*, and Florence after the Lady of the Lamp, Florence Nightingale, whose nursing at Scutari during the Crimean War was awarded with an Order of Merit.

In America, Lee, initially a boy's name, was first used in the Southern states of America in the 1860s in honour of the commander of the Confederate forces General Robert E Lee. General Lachlan Macquarie, much-loved Governor of New South Wales from 1809–21 was responsible for generations of Lachlans in Australia and is still in the top 30 Australian names.

During the Second World War, Winston was a popular choice in Holland in response to Nazi-occupied Holland, and reputedly one in eight Jordanian boys born during the Gulf War were named Saddam.

Peacetime brings different heroes. There are as likely to be footballers as generals or popstars. Classical heroic names have also made a comeback, such as Alexander, Hector, St George, Tibor and Zoltan. Will they prove inspirational?

Aithne (G)
English version of the Irish Aodhnait, meaning 'little fire'. A favourite name in Ireland for centuries, it is also written Aine or Eithne.

Alain (B)
French form of the ancient Breton Celtic name Alawn, meaning 'harmony'. A classic French name it has been adopted as an alternative spelling to Alan since the 50s.

Alan (B)
Modern English form of the ancient Celtic Alawn or Eilian, meaning 'harmony', a classic of the 20th century. The medieval spelling was Allan.

Alana (G)
Irish feminine form of Alan, meaning 'harmony'.

Alasdair (B)
Gaelic form of Alexander, meaning 'protector of men'. Alexander was introduced to Scotland in the 11th century and this Highlands version of the name had probably developed by the late Middle Ages, and came into English usage

in the 20th century. The alternative spelling is Alastair but the most popular form in Scotland at the moment is Alistair.

Albert (B)
German, with associations of 'noble' and 'bright'. The name was unknown in England until Queen Victoria married Prince Albert of Saxe-Coburg-Gotha in 1840. The popularity of the prince made it a favourite Victorian name.

Alberta (G)
Feminine form of Albert sometimes used in the 19th century. The French form, which is prettier, is Albertine.

Aldous (B)
French form of the Old German 'aldo' meaning 'old', perhaps with the association of wisdom.

Alec (B)
Scottish short form of Alexander meaning 'protector of men'; it is also spelt Alick.

Aleksandr (B)
Russian form of Alexander. The Russian feminine form is Aleksandrina.

Alethea (G)
Greek, meaning 'truth'. A literary name from the seventh century.

Alexander (B)
From Greek, meaning 'protector of men' and one of the great European and Asiatic royal names. It may well have been Hittite in origin, since the name of Hittite King Alaksandus has been found on a clay tablet dating from 1300 BC, but was adopted by the Greeks, and particularly by the Macedonians, for whom the names Alexander and Philip became hereditary. Alexander the Great (356–323 BC) is the most famous bearer of the name. Perhaps surprisingly, the greatest stronghold of the name in Britain has been Scotland where it has been in almost continuous use for 100 years. In the present century there has been an enthusiastic revival and is now in the top 20 boys' names.

Alexandra (G)
Russian feminine form of Alexander meaning 'protector of men' which came to popularity in the 19th century following the marriage of the Prince of Wales, later Edward VII, to Alexandra of Denmark.

Alexandrina (G)
Russian/Germanic diminutive of Alexandra, the first name of Queen Victoria, who was known as Drina as a child.

Alexis (B&G)
From Greek, meaning 'protector' or 'helper', used both as a name in its own right and as a short form of Alexander.

Alfred (B)
From Old English, with associations of 'elf' and 'counsel', a royal name famously born by Alfred the Great. It fell out of use after the Norman Conquest but was revived in the 19th century when there was a new interest in Saxon history.

Algernon (B)
Old French, from a nickname 'aux gernons' meaning 'the one with the whiskers'. It was the name of two counts of Boulogne in the 11th century who obviously had particularly fine examples! Adopted as a font name by the Percys of Northumberland it came into general use in the 19th century when there was a fashion for aristocratic names.

Alice (G)
From Old German, meaning 'nobility'. Enormously popular following the publication in 1865 of Lewis Carroll's *Alice's Adventures in Wonderland*, it is for many the quintessential Victorian name.

Alicia (G)
Latin form of Alice, meaning 'nobility', which was popular between the 12th and 17th centuries. Revived in the mid-19th century and occasionally found today.

Aline (G)
Old English form of Adeline, meaning 'nobility'. The Latin form was Alina which was popular in the Middle Ages. Aline was revived for its medieval feel in the 19th century.

Alisander (B)

Lowlands Scots of Alexander (the Highlands version is Alasdair) with the meaning 'protector of men'. Alexander was introduced to Scotland as early as the 11th century when Queen Margarete of Hungary married into the Scottish royal family and called her third son, who was to become king, Alysandyr. Sandy is the familiar form.

Alison (G)

Medieval pet-form of Alis or Alice which appears both in France and England in the 13th century; there is an Alison in Chaucer's *Canterbury Tales*. It was fairly common in England until the 17th century, particularly in the north, and especially so in Scotland.

Alix (G)

Old French, meaning 'nobility', it was also sometimes written Aliz. 'La belle Alix' was the wife of Henry I.

Allegra (G)

Italian, meaning 'cheerful'. One of the classic aristocratic Italian names.

Alma (G)

Italian, meaning 'soul'.

Aloisa (G)

French Provençal, meaning 'renowned warrior' and pronounced both Al-louisa and Aloy-sa. It is found in English parish registers of the 16th and 17th centuries.

Alon (B)

From Hebrew, meaning 'tree of life'.

Althea (G)

From Greek, meaning 'healthy' or 'wholesome'. It was a fashionable name in Stuart times when there was an interest in classical names.

Alvin (B)

German, meaning 'noble friend'.

Alvis (B)

Scandinavian, meaning 'all wise'. An alternative spelling is Elvis.

Alwyn (B)
Saxon name dating from the seventh century, meaning 'famous friend'.

Alys (G)
Welsh form of Alice meaning 'nobility'.

Amadeus (B)
Latin meaning 'beloved of the Gods'.

Amanda (G)
From Latin, meaning 'lovable' and coined by dramatists of the Restoration period although it did not come into general use until the present century. Noël Coward immortalized the name in his *Private Lives* (1933) and it was a favourite name in the 50s and 60s.

Amber (G)
Jewel name coined in the 60s which is tipped for popularity in the 90s through an association with the supermodel Amber Valetta. The name was first noted in the United States in the late 50s and was a popular name there in the late 80s, when it was given to one in 100 girls.

Ambrose (B)
From Greek, meaning 'immortal'.

Ambrosia (G)
Feminine form of Ambrose, from Greek, meaning 'immortal' and recorded as early as the 16th century.

Amelia (G)
From Old German, meaning 'hard work'. Although the name appears in Shakespeare's *The Comedy of Errors*, it did not come into general use until the 18th century when it was a favourite royal and court name of the Hanoverians. The Italian form is Emilia, from which Emily is derived.

Aminta (G)
Coined by the Restoration dramatist Sir John Vanbrugh from the Greek male name Amyntas, meaning 'defender' which had been a name used by the Macedonian royal family, to which Alexander the Great belonged, from the fourth century BC.

Amos (B)
Hebrew, meaning 'a burden' and the name of an Old Testament prophet.

Amy (G)
English form of the French Aimée, meaning 'beloved'. The first known Amy in England was Amy Robsart, wife of Robert Devereux, Earl of Essex, who was a favourite of Elizabeth I. It was a favourite name of the Pilgrim Fathers and has long enjoyed popularity in the United States. In the last few years it has enjoyed new popularity and is now in the top ten names for girls.

Anais (G)
French, from Greek, meaning 'fruitful'. Colette popularized the name by using it for one of the characters in her Claudine books. It is pronounced An-eye-eese.

Anastasia (G)
From Greek, meaning 'resurrection', one of the names of the early Eastern Orthodox Church, associated with a fourth-century saint, which also passed into Russian. Surprisingly it was found in England for many centuries as Anstey and Anastase. The Russian diminutive is Nastasya.

Anatole (B)
French, from Greek, meaning 'sunrise'.

André (B)
French version of Andrew.

Andrea (G)
Feminine form of Greek Andreas. Popular in the 17th century, it was revived at the end of the 19th century when there was a fashion for classical Greek and Roman names.

Andreas (B)
Ancient Greek name, found in papyri, meaning 'manly', and the name by which St Andrew was known until the Norman Conquest. It remains popular in both Greece and the Netherlands.

Andrée (G)
French feminine form of André, which has been in use in England since the 50s.

Celebrity children's names

Hollywood film-stars, rock and pop musicians and TV celebrities at the font

Moonunit, Dweezil, Ahmet and Diva (Frank Zappa's children)

Rummer Glenn, Scout LaRue, Tallulah Belle (Bruce Willis and Demi Moore's children)

Zowie (David Bowie's son)

Born Free (Barbara Hershey's son)

Sage Moonblood (Sylvester Stallone's son)

Chastity (Cher's daughter)

Dandelion (Keith Richards' daughter)

Satchell, Dylan (Mia Farrow's son and daughter)

God (Grace Slick's daughter)

Harvey Kirby, Betty Ritten (Jonathan Ross's son and daughter)

Fifi Trixie-belle, Peaches, Pixie (Bob Geldof and Paula Yates' daughters)

Zulekha (Iman's daughter)

Pleasingly the offspring occasionally fight back. Mia Farrow's seven-year-old son Satchell and nine-year-old daughter Dylan have changed their names to Seamus and Eliza, Dylan being tired of being mistaken for a boy. And by the age of 15, Barbara Hershey's son Born Free had finally had enough. He opted for Tom.

Andrew (B)

The name of the first disciple called by Jesus who preached in the Balkans and was put to death on a X-shaped cross. He is the patron saint of Russia and Scotland and his saint's day is 30 November. A popular name in Scotland since t⅂

Middle Ages, it was less common in England until the present century when a revival of interest in New Testament names in the 60s brought it into mainstream use again.

Andrina (G)
Russian shortened form of Aleksandrina. Queen Victoria was christened Alexandrina, but known as Drina for short.

Aneira (G)
Welsh, meaning 'all gold'.

Aneurin (B)
Old Welsh name, meaning 'all gold'. The seventh-century Aneurin ap Caw was one of the three great bards of Britain. The short form is Nye.

Angela (G)
Italian, from Latin, meaning 'angel'. Both Angela and Angel are found in medieval records. It was revived towards the end of the 19th century and was a popular name in the 50s.

Angelica (G)
From Latin, meaning 'angelic'. It was a popular Italian medieval name, but was not adopted in England until the 18th century. The French form is Angélique.

Angelina (G)
Italian diminutive of Angela, meaning 'angelic'.

Angharad (G)
Old Welsh, meaning 'much-loved' and a name which appears in Welsh legend. It came into English usage at the end of the 19th century when there was a revival of interest in the book of Old Welsh tales, *The Mabinogion*.

Angus (B)
English form of the Gaelic Aonghus, meaning 'unique choice'. The oldest recorded bearer was Aonghus Turimleach who invaded Scotland from Ireland in the third century BC. Long popular in the Highlands, it came into English use in the mid-19th century when there was a fashion for all things Scottish.

Aniela (G)
Italian, meaning 'angel' and pronounced An-eye-ella.

Anis (G)
Medieval form of Agnes, meaning 'pure'. It was also written Annis and Annice.

Anita (G)
Spanish diminutive of Anna, literally meaning 'little Anna'. Popular in England in the 50s.

Ann (G)
Medieval English form of the Latin Anna, meaning 'grace'. The Hebrew form is Hannah. It has been a classic English name for nearly 800 years.

Anna (G)
Greek and Latin form of the ancient Hebrew name Hannah, meaning 'grace'. The name has long royal and biblical associations, from the royal house of Carthage, to early saints, Byzantine empresses and Russian tsarinas. It was introduced to England from France in the 17th century and has been revived again since the 50s.

Annabel (G)
Scottish royal name, with the meaning of 'lovable'. The first recorded Annabel was the daughter of Duncan Earl of Moray in the 12th century, since when it has remained in use in aristocratic families in the Highlands. It came into use in England as a result of Edgar Allan Poe's poem 'Annabel Lee' (1849).

Anna Maria (G)
Spanish, with the associations of 'grace' and 'longed for' In scriptural legend Anna was the mother of the Virgin Mary.

Anne (G)
French form of Latin Anna, meaning 'grace', which in turn comes from the Hebrew Hannah. Anne was introduced from France in the 13th century and was quickly adopted as a noble and royal name. In the 19th century it was temporarily superseded by Anna, but has returned to be a firm favourite of the 20th century.

Annette (G)
French diminutive of Anne, meaning 'little graceful one', which has been in England since the end of the 19th century.

Annie (G)
Scottish pet-form of Anne.

Annika (G)
Scandinavian diminutive of Anne, meaning 'little graceful one'. It is also spelt Anneka.

Annona (G)
From Latin, meaning 'harvest'. The Welsh form is Annwen.

Anthea (G)
Greek, meaning 'lady of the flowers'. The Latin name is Flora. It was first brought into English usage as a poetic name in the 17th century and was revived at the end of the 19th century for its classical associations.

Anthony (B)
From Latin Antonius, meaning 'praise-worthy', and the name of one of the great and wealthy patrician families of Ancient Rome. The purest form is Antony, but the 'th' crept in in the 16th century and has stayed there.

Antoinette (G)
French feminine form of Antony which has come into English usage. It has the associated meaning of 'little praise-worthy one'.

Anton (B)
Russian form of Antony which came into use at the end of the 19th century when there was a fashion for Russian names.

Antonia (G)
From Latin, meaning 'inestimable'. It was adopted from Italian usage in the 19th century.

Antony (B)
From Latin Antonius, meaning 'praise-worthy' and the name of one of the great patrician families of Ancient Rome. There were two St Antonys: St Antony of Egypt and St Antony of Padua.

Anwen (G)
Welsh, meaning 'very beautiful'.

Aphra (G)
From Hebrew, meaning 'dust'. The name was revived from the Old Testament Book of Micah by the Puritans in the

17th century. The most famous bearer of the name was the early novelist Aphra Behn.

April (G)
Edwardian month name.

Arabella (G)
Scottish noble and royal name, possibly from the Latin 'orabilis', meaning 'prayerful'. It was a royal Stuart name.

Araminta (G)
Coined by the Restoration dramatists and an aristocratic and literary 17th-century name, with the meaning 'prayer' and 'protection'.

Archibald (B)
From Old German, meaning 'genuine' and 'bold'. A favourite Scottish name since the reign of James I, particularly among the Cameron and Douglas clans. Scott's *A Legend of Montrose* (1819), with its hero Archie Armstrong, brought it into favour in England.

Ariane (G)
Greek, meaning 'very holy one'. The modern Greek version is Arianna.

Ariel (B&G)
Hebrew, meaning 'lion of God'. The Italian version of the girl's name is Ariella.

Aristotle (B)
Greek, meaning 'best thinker', still extremely popular in Greece, especially the short form, Telly.

Arleen (G)
From Celtic Irish, meaning 'pledge'. An alternative spelling, which is favoured in the United States is Arlene.

Arnold (B)
Old German, meaning 'power of the eagle'. It came into use after the Norman Conquest and was popular in the 12th and 13th centuries. The Victorians revived it for its historical associations but also in admiration of Dr Arnold of Rugby and his son, Matthew Arnold, the poet.

Art (B)
American short form of Arthur.

Scottish names

The Registrar General for Scotland's surveys of Scottish Christian names for 1858, 1935, 1958, 1976 and 1990 show that Margaret, Mary and Elizabeth held the top three positions for girls in the 100 years from 1858 and John, James and William the top three positions for boys. The pool of names in use for this period was relatively small, rising from a few hundred to less than a thousand for both girls and boys.

In 1990, Scottish parents were choosing from 2,679 girls' names and 1,518 boys' names. Girls' names in particular come from a wide range of sources and include Jade, Kayleigh, Ashleigh, Natasha, Siobhan, Leanne, Melissa, Hayley, Holly, Kirsten, Robyn, Michaela and Aimee. Boys' names are generally more conservative, but new names include Liam, Jordan, Lewis, Marc, Kieran, Jason, Aaron, Joshua, Dale and Connor.

Top boys' names for 1993:

Andrew	1 in 30	Daniel	1 in 51
Ryan	1 in 36	Jamie	1 in 53
David	1 in 36	John	1 in 60
Scott	1 in 39	Steven	1 in 64
James	1 in 42	Sean	1 in 68
Michael	1 in 42	Mark	1 in 69
Christopher	1 in 42	Liam	1 in 74
Ross	1 in 43	Lewis	1 in 81
Craig	1 in 47	Stuart	1 in 81
Jordan	1 in 50	Matthew	1 in 83

Top girls' names for 1993:

Emma	1 in 39	Nicole	1 in 53
Rebecca	1 in 41	Rachel	1 in 56
Lauren	1 in 44	Stephanie	1 in 64
Laura	1 in 46	Hannah	1 in 67
Amy	1 in 48	Jennifer	1 in 67
Sarah	1 in 51	Kirsty	1 in 69

Megan	1 in 69	Samantha	1 in 84
Danielle	1 in 76	Gemma	1 in 86
Claire	1 in 80	Lisa	1 in 93
Nicola	1 in 82	Natalie	1 in 97

Names of Scottish origin appearing in the top 100:

Boys: Callum and Calum, Graeme, Iain, Fraser, Gavin, Ian, Gordon, Neil, Stewart, Euan, Kyle, Alistair, Cameron, Ewan, Duncan, Rory, Alasdair, Niall, Donald, Murray, Keith.

Girls: Fiona, Heather, Eilidh, Jenna, Catriona, Mhairi, Alison.

Artemis (G)
Greek goddess of the moon, hunting and the woodlands. Her Roman counterpart was Diana.

Artemisia (G)
Greek, the name given to the Queen of Caria who built the Mausoleum at Halicarnassus, one of the seven wonders of the ancient world. Popular in the south London boroughs of Lewisham, Greenwich and Bermondsey in the 16th century.

Arthur (B)
From Ancient Welsh 'arth gwr', meaning 'bear hero', suggesting it was a royal name even before King Arthur's time. Its Celtic roots, going back 1,000 years BC, mean it also appears in Irish and Scottish legend. Out of use after the Norman Conquest, it was revived by the Welsh Henry Tudor, who became Henry VII who christened his first son Arthur. In the 19th century, the popularity of Arthur Wellesley Duke of Wellington revived its fortunes.

Asa (B)
Hebrew, meaning 'healer' or 'physician'.

Ashley (B&G)
English surname which has become a Christian name in the
20th century. Its popularity may have been boosted by Leslie
Howard's portrayal of Ashley Wilkes in the 1939 classic
Gone with the Wind. It is now in the top 20 names for boys
and in the United States has been in the top ten for girls.

Astra (G)
Greek, meaning 'star'. The diminutive is Astrella.

Astrid (G)
Norse, meaning 'strength of god' and a favourite name of
the royal families of Scandinavia for centuries.

Atalanta (G)
Italian, from Greek, and the name of the mythical daughter
of Iasus whose swiftness of foot was legendary.

Athena (G)
Greek, the name of the goddess of wisdom.

Auberon (B)
From French, meaning 'little Aubrey', a diminutive which
came into use in England in the 13th century. In folklore
it is associated with the mischievous King of the Fairies.

Aubrey (B)
English form of French Aubert, meaning 'elf-rule'. Popular
in the Middle Ages, it passed out of use but was revived in
the 19th century for its medieval feel.

Audrey (G)
Short form of Anglo-Saxon Etheldreda which was in use
from the seventh to the 16th century. Revived in the 19th
century for its Old-English feel, it remains popular.

Augusta (G)
Latin, meaning 'sacred' or 'venerable', the title given to
wives and daughters of Roman emperors. In the 16th
century, it became a fashionable royal and princely christening name in Germany and was introduced to England
at the Hanoverian court in the 18th century.

Augustus (B)
Latin, meaning 'majesty', the title given to Roman emperors. It was introduced to England by the Hanoverians,

having become a well-established royal name in Germany. It shares its short form Gus with Angus.

Aurora (G)
Roman goddess of the dawn. The French form Aurore has been a popular name since the 16th century.

Austin (B)
Short form of Augustine, meaning 'venerable' which was common in the Middle Ages. It was revived in the 19th century by Tractarians for its religious associations.

Ava (G)
Form of German Eva coined after the actress Ava Gardner.

Aveline (G)
From Old German, meaning 'hazel', the hazel being the ancient European fruit of wisdom. It was introduced to England by the Normans and was much in use in the Middle Ages. The novelist Fanny Burney revived the Latin form for her novel *Evelina* (1778).

Averil (G)
Anglo-Saxon name associated with Yorkshire. St Everild founded a nunnery in the county in the seventh century. By the 17th century the name had reached its present form and is still in use, particularly in the north of England.

Avril (G)
French, meaning 'April'. In this century it has been used for girls born during that month.

Axel (B)
Scandinavian, meaning 'divine reward'.

Ayesha (G)
From Arabic Aisha, meaning 'woman' and the name of the favourite wife of the prophet Mohammed. It was sometimes used as a christian name following the publication of Rider Haggard's *She* in 1887.

B

Babette (G)
French pet form of Elisabeth, literally 'little Elizabeth'.

Babs (G)
Short form of Barbara dating from the 17th century.

Balthasar (B)
Babylonian, meaning 'God protect the King'. Balthasar was one of the names associated in medieval legend with the Three Kings or Magi.

Banquo (B)
From Gaelic, meaning 'white' or 'fair'.

Barbara (G)
From Greek, meaning 'foreigner'. St Barbara was one of the four great women saints – the others were Margaret, Agnes and Katherine – of the early Christian world. Popular in the Middle Ages, it then fell out of use until this century when it has become a favourite.

Barnabas (B)
Aramaic, meaning 'son of exhortation'. Barnabas was an apostle and companion of St Paul on his travels.

Barnaby (B)
English form of Barnabas which has been in use for more than six centuries.

Barry (B)
From Irish Bearrach, meaning 'spear', an ancient Celtic name, and the name of a sixth-century Irish saint. In the form Barry, it came into English usage in the 19th century, popularized by Thackeray's novel, *The Adventures of Barry Linden*.

Bart (B)
Shortened form of Bartholomew and Bartley, a name in its own right in America.

Baby boom

The birthrate in Britain has remained remarkably static since the 1920s, with, on average, 740,000 babies being born each year in England, Scotland and Wales.

There have been two notable peaks when the birthrate rose to nearly a million, once in 1947 following the conclusion of the Second World War (994,173) and once in 1964 (980,327), the latter occurring midway through the famous 60s' 'baby boom'. Troughs have reflected times of national anxiety: the depression years of the early 1930s (666,959 in 1933), wartime (668,839 in 1941) and economic recession (653,154 in 1976). Birthrate as an indicator of national mood would seem to suggest that the recession of the late 1980s bit less deep than suggested. The number of babies born rose steadily through the 1980s and the latest figures available for 1992 show it stands at 755,447 with projections of a five per cent increase until the year 2000.

1928	757,609
1938	709,831
1948	875,650
1958	840,196
1961	912,430
1968	914,059
1978	660,713
1981	703,536
1988	759,789
1990	773,169

Bartholomew (B)
Hebrew 'Bar Talmai', literally 'Son of the furrow'. Bartholomew was one of the Apostles. The name was made famous in the Middle Ages by St Bartholomew, who founded the hospital in London and had 165 churches dedicated to him.

Bartley (B)
Shortened form of Bartholomew that became a name in its own right. In the north of England it is Bartle.

Basil (B)
From Greek, meaning 'king'. Basil was the name of three great eastern saints and several Byzantine emperors. It was brought West during the Crusades and found particular favour with the Scots as a substitute for their Gaelic name, Boisil. It was a popular Victorian and Edwardian name.

Basilia (G)
Feminine form of Basil used in the Middle Ages.

Bathsheba (G)
Hebrew, meaning 'daughter of an oath'. The story of Bathsheba, who became David's second wife, is told in the Book of Samuel. Her name was used in the Middle Ages and beyond. Bathsheba Everdene in Thomas Hardy's *Far from the Madding Crowd* (1874) is the best known literary evocation of her name.

Bea (G)
Short form of Beatrice or Beatrix.

Bearrach (B)
Ancient Celtic name, meaning 'good marksman'. It passed into Irish as Bearach, meaning 'sword'.

Beata (G)
Italian, meaning 'happy' or 'blessed', it is pronounced Bay-arta.

Beatrice (G)
Italian, meaning 'bestower of blessings'. History's most celebrated Beatrice is the Italian poet, Dante's, Beatrice Portinari, whom he called 'the glorious lady of my heart';

they met when he was ten and she nine. Italian names were popular in the 16th century and Shakespeare produces a Beatrice in *Much Ado About Nothing*, but the name subsequently fell into disuse. In the mid-19th century, it was revived as a royal name. Queen Victoria's youngest daughter was christened Beatrice and it became a popular Victorian and Edwardian christening name. In the 80s it found favour again when the Duke and Duchess of York called their elder child Beatrice.

Beatrix (G)
Latin, meaning 'bestower of blessings'. This was the medieval form of Beatrice, brought to England by the Normans and a fairly common name in the Middle Ages. It was revived in the fashion for classical names at the end of the 19th century.

Becky (G)
Short form of Rebecca dating back to the 19th century. Becky Sharpe appears in Thackeray's *Vanity Fair* (1847).

Bede (B)
Anglo-Saxon, meaning 'prayer'. The name is associated with the first recorder of English history, the Venerable Bede.

Belinda (G)
Originally a Frankish name, meaning 'sacred serpent', it was not known in England until the Restoration when playwrights were taken with pretty feminine names. Alexander Pope made Belinda the heroine of his poem 'The Rape of the Lock' (1712) and Congreve, Vanbrugh and Tate also adopted the name. Although popular in the 18th century, it did not survive as a Victorian name, although it has been in steady used in the present century.

Bella (G)
Literally, Italian for 'beautiful', it is used as a short form of Isabella and Arabella. The French form is Belle.

Ben (B)
Short form of Benjamin and Benedict which has been in use since the Middle Ages.

Benedick (B)
Form of Benedict used by Shakespeare in *Much Ado About Nothing*.

Benedict (B)
Latin, 'benedictus', meaning 'blessed'. St Benedict founded a monastic order in the fifth century which spread across Europe. The name was brought to England at the time of the Norman Conquest and enjoyed some popularity in the Middle Ages and 16th century before falling into disuse. It has been revived quite handsomely in the 20th century.

Benedicta (G)
Feminine form of Benedict, meaning 'blessed'. The French form is Benedicte.

Benita (G)
Spanish form of Benedicta which is immensely popular in Spanish-speaking South America. It means 'blessed'.

Benjamin (B)
From Hebrew, meaning 'son of the right hand'. Jacob called his last born child Benjamin, as the story is told in the Old Testament. The Puritans revived the name and, with the short form Ben, it came more or less into continual use from the 16th century. In France 'le benjamin' or 'la benjamine' is the term for the youngest child.

Berenice (G)
From Greek, meaning 'bringer of victory'. Berenice was a royal name, used by the Ptolemy dynasty of Egypt as a name for wives and daughters, in the same way that Candace was used as a title for the queens of Ethiopia. The name also passed into the Herod family where it appears in the Bible as an honorary name for princesses.

Bernadette (G)
French feminine form of Bernard, with the same meaning, 'resolution of a bear', because bears were considered sacred in early times. The popularity of the name, particularly in France and Ireland, derives from the fame of St Bernadette of Lourdes who lived from 1844 to 1879.

Bernard (B)
From Anglo-Saxon and Old-German, meaning 'resolution

The call of the sea

The ancient language of the Celts, from which Irish and Scottish Gaelic, Manx, Welsh and Cornish are derived, was rich in lyrically descriptive names. The language was a cousin of ancient Greek and Sanskrit and as such personal names were drawn from the natural world or formed from elements of the names of the gods and goddesses who maintained the rhythm of the seasons and order of the heavens. When the Celts were pushed into the western extremities of Europe by the Anglo-Saxons 1,400 years ago, their separate kingdoms were joined only by the sea and they consequently became great sea-faring people. The following names originated in the old Celtic word for sea, 'myr'.

Meraud (G)
Cornish, meaning 'little one of the sea'

Meriel (G)
Norman-Breton, meaning 'sheen of the sea'

Meryl (G)
Welsh, meaning 'sea-bright'

Morgan (B)
Welsh, meaning 'sea-born'

Morvoren (G)
Cornish, meaning 'maid of the sea' or 'mermaid'

Murdoch (B)
From Gaelic Muirdeadhach', meaning 'sea leader'

Muriel (G)
Norman-Breton, meaning 'sheen of the sea'

Murray (B)
Scottish surname from place name meaning 'sea'

---

of a bear'. Bears were regarded as sacred creatures in many European cultures and both the Scandinavian Bjorn and Celtic Arth have much the same meaning. Bernard was revived in the 19th century.

Bernice (G)
Short form of Berenice, meaning 'bringer of victory'. It is popular in the United States, both for its biblical associations and for its origin as a title of princesses and queens.

Bertha (G)
Old Frankish name, meaning 'bright'. In Austria it is given to girls born on 6 January, the festival night for the legendary goddess Berchta. It was occasionally used in England in the 19th century. There has been a revival of the form Berthe, pronounced Bear-te, in France since the 70s.

Bertie (B)
Affectionate form of Albert associated with the Royal family.

Bertram (B)
From Old German, meaning 'bright raven'. The French form is Bertrand.

Beryl (G)
Persian and Arabic name, meaning 'crystal'. A very old name, which only came into use in England at the end of the 19th century. It was adopted as a jewel name and its popularity soared following the publication of a racy novel called *Beryl Molozone*.

Bess (G)
Short form of Elizabeth popular in Elizabethan and Jacobean times among the aristocracy.

Beth (G)
Short form of Elizabeth used by the Puritans and taken to the United States in the 17th century where it still flourishes.

Bethan (G)
Welsh pet form of Elizabeth, meaning 'little Elizabeth'.

Bettina (G)
Italian form of Elizabeth which was sometimes used as

a Christian name in the 19th century when there was a fashion for Italian names.

Betty (G)
Pet form of Elizabeth which was immensely popular as a Christian name in the 20s.

Beulah (G)
Hebrew name, used in the Old Testament, meaning 'married'.

Beverley (B&G)
At the turn of the century, Beverley was a boy's name derived from a family surname, which itself came from a place name in Yorkshire. By the 50s it had become a popular girl's name.

Bevis (B)
An Old Frankish name meaning 'ox'. It was an aristocratic and kingly name introduced to England by the Normans but had fallen out of use by the 13th century. Revived at the end of the 19th century by a children's book, *Bevis, the Story of a Boy*, it has been in occasional use since.

Bianca (G)
Italian, meaning 'fair-complexioned'. The Spanish form is Blanca.

Bibiana (G)
A variation of Viviana, the feminine form of Vivian, meaning 'lively'.

Biddy (G)
Affectionate form of Bridget used in Ireland. St Bridget, or St Bride as she is also known, was one of the great Irish saints.

Bjorn (B
Scandinavian, meaning 'bear'. The English equivalent is Bernard.

Blake (B)
Anglo-Saxon surname, probably meaning 'dark-complexioned'. Used as a Christian name in the present century.

Blanca (G)
Old Spanish, meaning 'fair', and the name of a famous

Names from the sub-continent

Hindu and Muslim names derive from Sanskrit, the classical Indian language which is also the oldest of the Indo-European family of languages (although Urdu, the language of Pakistan, also borrows heavily from Arabic and Persian) and are some of the most beautiful and ancient in the world. In the Hindu tradition the naming ceremony of a child is held twelve days after birth and the name chosen after the casting of horoscopes and conferring with family elders. In Muslim families the father reads the Asazan, or affirmation of belief in the Prophet, over the child. Boys are given a first name which is likely to be a traditional name within the family, for example all eldest sons may be called Abdul, and a second name by which the child will be known. Girls are known, instead, by their first name which is chosen more freely.

Boys

Aftab 'the sun'
Amal 'unblemished'
Amir 'rich'
Amrit 'nectar'
Anand 'joy'
Arun/Aroon 'charioteer of the sun'
Ashok 'without grief'
Farhad 'happiness'
Haroon 'hope'
Hemendu 'golden moon'
Imran 'strong'
Kamal 'lotus'
Kareem 'kind'
Khalid 'immortal'
Kiran 'ray of light'
Kumar 'prince'

Kuldeep 'light of family'
Madhu 'honey'
Madhur 'sweet'
Manik 'ruby'
Marut 'the wind'
Nadir 'the pinnacle'
Naresh 'king'
Nirad 'cloud'
Pavan 'breeze'
Pran 'life'
Prem 'love'
Priyam 'beloved'
Quamar 'moon'
Rahul 'son of lord Buddha'
Raj 'kingdom'
Rajan 'king'

Rajiv 'lotus'
Rakesh 'moon'
Ravi 'the sun'
Ravindra 'the sun'
Rohan 'ascending'
Roshan 'illumination'
Saeed 'priestly'
Sanjay 'charioteer'

Satish 'victorious'
Suhail 'moon-glow'
Tariq 'morning star'
Umed 'hope'
Utpal 'lotus'
Varun 'lord of the sea'
Vijay 'victory'
Zahid 'intelligent'

Girls

Adhira 'lightning'
Amala 'pure one'
Angarika 'flame of the forest'
Anshula 'sunny'
Aruna 'dawn'
Aruni 'dawn'
Ayesha 'daughter of the Prophet'
Beli or Bela 'jasmine'
Esha 'desire'
Geena 'silvery'
Heera 'diamond'
Keshi 'woman with beautiful hair'
Kokila 'cuckoo'
Laksha 'white rose'
Lalita 'beautiful'
Lata 'a creeper'
Madhur 'sweet'
Malati 'creeper with beautiful flowers'
Malika 'a garland'
Maya 'illusion'
Meena 'precious blue stone'
Naseen 'cool breeze'

Neela 'blue'
Nikhita 'earth'
Nisha 'night'
Noor 'light'
Noorjehan 'light of the world'
Nusrat 'help'
Parvani 'full moon'
Parveen 'star'
Pramila 'Arjuna's wife'
Rani 'queen'
Rupa 'silver'
Saeeda 'priestly'
Sanjula 'beautiful'
Savita 'the sun'
Sita 'wife of Lord Rama'
Suhaila 'moon-glow'
Suraiya 'beautiful'
Tasneem 'salute of paradise'
Usha 'dawn'
Ushashi 'morning'
Zareen 'golden'
Zarina 'queen'
Zulekha 'beautiful'

Queen of Castile. Her granddaughter was ... he bride for Louis VIII of France on account of ... y name.

Blanche (G)
French form of Blanca, meaning 'fair'. It fell out of fashion at the end of the Middle Ages, but has been revived in France recently for its romantic medieval feel.

Blodwen (G)
Welsh, meaning 'white flower'.

Blossom (G)
Pretty flower name which dates from the end of the 19th century and which is well established in the United States.

Bonita (G)
From Latin, meaning 'good'. It is a popular Spanish name.

Bonnie (G)
Scottish form of Bonita, meaning 'good' and with the association of 'pretty'.

Boris (B)
Old Slavic, from 'borotj', meaning 'fight', indicating it was a name for the noble and knightly classes. It is one of the few male Russian names that has taken root in the West.

Bradley (B)
American name derived from an Anglo-Saxon surname, the short form being Brad.

Bram (B)
Short form of Abraham, most famously associated with Bram Stoker, christened Abraham, who wrote *Dracula*.

Branwen (G)
Welsh, meaning 'raven-haired beauty'. In Welsh legend Branwen was the daughter of King Llyr and was renowned as 'the fairest damsel in the world'. She is thought to have been buried on Anglesey.

Brenda (G)
Shetland name from the Old Norse, meaning 'sword'. It became popular following Scott's novel *The Pirate* (1821).

Brendan (B)
English form of the Irish Brenainn, the name of one Ireland's great saints who founded a monastery at Clonfert in the sixth century.

Brian (B)
Celtic, from 'brigh', meaning 'strength'. It appears in both Irish and Breton legend as the name of warriors and kings and was in continuous use until the 16th century. Revived in the present century for its Celtic origins and romantic feel, it has become something of a classic.

Brice (B)
From Old French and the name of an early saint. St Brice was Bishop of Tours in the fifth century and his name survived well into the Middle Ages. It was revived at the end of the 19th century.

Bríd (G)
Irish, meaning 'the high one'. It is pronounced Bree-da.

Bridget (G)
English form of the ancient Celtic Brighid, or Brid, meaning 'the high one' who in Irish legend was the daughter of the sun-god. St Bridget of Kildare is, with St Patrick and St Columba, one of the three great Irish saints and Bridget has been a favourite name in Ireland for centuries.

Bridgid (G)
In Celtic legend, Brighid was the daughter of the sun-god and this is closest to the original spelling of her name.

Bridie (G)
Charming Scottish diminutive of Bridget which originated from Brid, the Irish Gaelic form of Bridget.

Brigitta (G)
From the Swedish, with the associations of 'mountain' and 'protection', and a popular name there from the 14th century.

Brigitte (G)
French form of the Swedish Brigitta which dates from the Middle Ages.

Britain, Brittany is now the most popular name
ited States and has been in the top ten since the
80s.

Bronwen (G)
Welsh, with the meaning of 'white breast', suggesting it was a royal name. It was adopted by the English at the turn of the century.

Bronya (G)
Russian, meaning 'armour'.

Bruce (B)
Originally the name of a Norman feudal family; its association with Scotland dates from the fame of Robert the Bruce in the 14th century, although it was not in general use until the 19th century.

Brunilla (G)
Pretty Italian version of the Germanic Brunhilda, meaning 'battle maid'.

Bruno (B)
Italian, meaning 'brown', probably in reference to the colour of someone's eyes or hair.

Bryan (B)
Irish spelling of the Old Celtic name Brien or Brian, meaning 'strength', popular in the present century.

Bryony (G)
The name of an English plant which has been used as a Christian name in the last 30 years.

Burt (B)
American form of Bert and a short form of Burton, a surname which has become a Christian name.

Byron (B)
Lord Byron's fame in the 19th century resulted in the use of his name as a Christian name for its aristocratic associations.

C

Caitlin (G)
Modern Irish form of Catherine. The medieval Irish spelling was Catlin, which also reflects the true pronunciation.

Callum (B)
From Gaelic form of Columba, or Colm, meaning 'dove'. Both Callum and Calum have been in use in Scotland for many years, but recently the fashion for the name has spread south of the border. It is already tipped as one of the names for the 90s.

Calypso (G)
In Greek mythology the name of the queen of the island of Ogygia (thought to be Gozo, the island off the coast of Malta) who kept the wanderer Ulysses entranced for seven years. Mary Wesley borrowed the name for her *fille fatale* in *The Camomile Lawn*.

Candace (G)
From Assyrian, meaning 'majesty'. It was the honorary title of the queens of Ethiopia.

Candia (G)
Greek, the old name for Heraklion in Crete, sometimes used as a Christian name.

Candida (G)
From Latin, meaning 'fair-complexioned'. There was a tenth-century St Candida of Dorset, but the name was not in use until the very end of the 19th century, popularized by George Bernard Shaw's play, *Candida* (1897).

Cara (G)
Italian, meaning 'dear' or 'beloved'.

Carey (B&G)
Great Elizabethan family name, originally written Carew, which, like Cecil and Percy, came into use as a boy's

Christian name in the 19th century for its aristocratic associations. In the second half of the present century it has also become popular for girls.

Carl (B)
From Old German 'ceorl', meaning 'a man' and a name which has been in more or less constant use in the German language since the fifth century. In the last century when there was a fashion for names of German origin.

Carla (G)
Italian feminine form of Carlo, or Charles. The diminutive is Carlotta.

Carlo (B)
Italian form of Charles which dates from the 12th century.

Carmen (G)
Spanish form of Hebrew 'carmel', meaning 'garden', and the name of an important saint. The most famous Carmen is Bizet's, the feisty heroine of his opera, based on Mérimée's story.

Carol (G)
Feminine form of Charles which first appeared in the 17th century as Carola when it was a name traditionally given to daughters of Royalists during the Civil War. The short form Carol seems to have developed in the United States and came into use in England in the 30s. It was a popular name in the 50s.

Carole (G)
Form of Carol, popularized by Carole Lombard who was given her name by MGM in the 30s.

Caroline (G)
English form of German Carolina which came into fashion in England through its association with Carolina of Ansbach, wife of George II who became queen in 1727. It was a favourite 18th-century name and happily has been revived in the present century.

Carolyn (G)
Modern form of Caroline which has appeared since the 50s.

Carys (G)
Welsh, meaning 'love'.

Casimir (B)
Polish royal and noble name, meaning 'proclamation of peace'.

Caspar (B)
From Persian, meaning 'master of the treasure'. Caspar, Melchior and Balthasar were the names given to the Three Wise Men who 'came from the East' to pay homage to the infant Jesus. Caspar is the German, Gaspard the French and Jasper the English form of the name.

Cassandra (G)
In Greek mythology Cassandra was the daughter of King Priam and Queen Hecuba of Troy and had the gift of fortelling the future. A common name in the Middle Ages when tales of the ancient Greeks were celebrated by travelling poets, it was revived again in the 17th and 18th centuries. Jane Austen's sister was called Cassandra.

Castor (B)
Greek, meaning 'the beaver'. Castor and Pollux were the heavenly twins of Zeus.

Caterina (G)
Italian form of Katherine, which derived from the Greek Aikaterine, the original form of Katherine.

Catharine (G)
From Greek 'katharos', meaning 'pure', which came to be the associated meaning of the old name Aikaterine, or Katherine.

Catherine (G)
English form of the Italian Caterina, which itself derives from the Greek Aikaterine, an ancient name which was the original form of Katherine. Never out of fashion from the 16th century, Catherine has been the form favoured by parents for the last two centuries.

Catrin (G)
Welsh form of Catherine.

Catriona (G)
Scottish form of Catherine which was brought to a general public by Robert Louis Stevenson who wrote a sequel to *Kidnapped* called *Catriona* (1893). An increasingly popular Christian name in Scotland, it is correctly pronounced Ca-trear-na. The Irish Gaelic form is Caitríona.

Cecil (B)
From Latin, the name of a great Roman family, the Caecilii, or 'blind ones', probably after a founding member of the clan. It appears in medieval records as a name for both girls and boys but subsequently fell into disuse. It was revived in the 19th century for its classical feel and for its aristocratic associations with one of the great landed families of England, the Cecils.

Cecilia (G)
From Latin, the name of a great Roman family. St Cecilia, patron saint of music and musicians, was martyred in the third century and became an immensely popular figure. Her saint's day is 22 November. William the Conqueror had a daughter called Cecilia. It became a favourite 18th-century name after Fanny Burney's novel *Cecilia* (1782).

Cecily (G)
English diminutive of Cecilia pronounced Sis-ley, it was a popular name in the Middle Ages and was revived in the 19th century for its medieval feel.

Cedric (B)
From Old Welsh Cedrych, meaning 'pattern of bounty' and the name chosen by Sir Walter Scott for the father of his eponymous hero, Ivanhoe (1819). It is extremely rare now.

Ceit (G)
Modern spelling of Kate which owes something to the Irish Gaelic.

Celeste (G)
French from Latin, meaning 'heavenly'. It was a common 19th-century French name and has a certain charm.

Celia (G)
From Etruscan Celi, meaning 'September' and the name of an important Roman family. It was a favourite Elizabethan

name, appearing at the font, in poetry and literature and was in regular use until the 18th century when it was eclipsed by Cecilia. The French form is Célie.

Celina (G)
From French Céline, the name of an early saint. It appears in medieval records in England.

Ceridwen (G)
Name of the Welsh goddess of poetic inspiration.

Ceris (G)
Welsh, meaning 'love'. It is pronounced Care-is.

Chad (B)
Celtic, the name of the monk of Lindisfarne who became a saint in the seventh century. His name was revived at the end of the last century.

Charity (G)
Puritan virtue name meaning 'love', the original meaning of 'caritas' in the Bible. Triplets were traditionally called Faith, Hope and Charity.

Charlemagne (B)
Latin, literally 'Charles the Great' and the name of the first Holy Roman Emperor who was crowned at Aachen on Christmas Day 800 AD.

Charles (B)
Anglo-Saxon and Old German name, meaning 'a man'. It has been a name with royal associations across Europe from the eighth century. There have been ten kings of France and 15 kings of Sweden called Charles, to say nothing of dukes, barons and counts. Through its association with the Stuart kings it lost popularity in the 17th century, but was revived again in the 19th and has stayed in the top 50 names since.

Charley (B)
English familiar form of Charles, sometimes used for girls called Charlotte.

Charlie (B)
Scottish familiar form of Charles.

— 37 —

Charlotte (G)

French form of the Italian Carlotta. It came to England with the Hanoverian kings in the 18th century, very much a royal name for princesses. In the early 19th century it was pronounced Char-lot-en, the pronunciation Char-lot coming much later. Quite rare in the first half of this century, it has been back in fashion from the 60s and now holds a comfortable place in the top ten names for girls.

Charmaine (G)

Modern form of Charmian, from Greek, meaning 'joy'. Charmian appears as Cleopatra's maidservant in Shakespeare's *Antony and Cleopatra*.

Chelsea (G)

Name of a district of London which has been used as a Christian name since the 60s. Popular in the United States for a number of years, it is now appearing in Britain's most popular name lists and is tipped as a name for the 90s.

Cherry (G)

Pet name for Charity which dates from 18th century.

Cheryl (G)

Welsh, meaning 'love'. A popular Christian name in the 50s and 60s.

Chesney (B)

French, meaning 'oak grove'.

Chloë (G)

Greek, meaning 'a young green shoot', often associated in mythology with the countryside. It also appears in the New Testament. St Paul converted a woman named Chloë. It is pronounced Clo-ee.

Christabel (G)

From Latin, meaning 'fair follower of Christ'. It is a very old name and appeared in an early English ballad, where Christabelle was the daughter of a 'bonnie King of Ireland'. Coleridge revived the name for his poem.

Christian (B&G)

From Latin, literally 'a Christian'. It is a popular boy's name in France and in Denmark has been the name of ten Danish kings. It was a girl's name in the Middle Ages.

Royal names of the ancient world

Vashti   Queen of Persia, the wife of Ahasuerus, she appears in the Book of Esther in the Old Testament

Shireen   Queen of Persia

Dido   Also called Elissa, the legendary daughter of Belus of Tyre and founder Queen of Carthage *c.* 1250 BC

Berenice   Royal name of the wives and daughters of the Ptolemy dynasty who ruled Egypt from 323 to 48 BC. It means 'bringer of victory'

Candace   Royal title of the ancient queens of Ethiopia

Cleopatra   Name of several queens of the Ptolemaic dynasty of Egypt, the most famous being Queen Cleopatra VII 69–30 BC, wife of Mark Antony

Zenobia   Queen of Palmyra, Syria 267–72, who was noted for her beauty

Jezebel   Phoenician princess who married King Ahab of Israel

Mehetabel   Wife of Hadar, King of Edom

Tamar   Royal name of the House of David, which was given to both the daughter and granddaughter of David. The Russian form is Tamara

Calypso   Legendary Queen of Ogygia who kept Ulysses entranced for seven years on her island. Calypso's cave is said to be on the island of Gozo in the Mediterranean.

Christine (G)
From Greek 'chrio', meaning 'I anoint'. The medieval form of Christine was Christian, used for girls and boys, but the popularity of Christine in present times is due to the fashion for the Italian Christina in the 19th century.

Christopher (B)
From Greek, meaning 'Christ-bearer' in reference to the patron saint of travellers and wayfarers who, according to legend, carried the infant Christ across the river. It appears in records in England in the 13th century and had established itself properly by Shakespeare's time, with the charming diminutive Kit. It was not a popular Victorian name, but has been regularly in use this century, experiencing something of a boom at the present time.

Chrystal (B)
Surprisingly, a Lowland Scot rendition of Christopher going back many centuries.

Chuck (B)
American short form of Charles.

Cicely (G)
Old English form of Cecily.

Cilla (G)
Short form of Priscilla and Lucilla, coined in the 20th century. Priscilla appears in the New Testament, and has the meaning of 'ancient'.

Cindy (G)
Short form of Lucinda coined in the 20th century.

Claire (G)
French version of the Italian Clara which became the favoured spelling of the name in England in the 60s. The true English form is Clare.

Clare (G)
From Italian, meaning 'clear' or 'bright'. St Clare of Assisi was a friend of St Francis and founded a religious order called the Poor Clares. It was a medieval name, but in subsequent centuries was preferred in more fanciful variations, such as Clarinda, Claribel and Clarissa. Clara was popular in the 19th century.

Clarence (B)
Royal name which came into use when a son of Edward III married an heiress from the Clare family of Suffolk. A Clarence Harvey in Maria Edgeworth's novel *Helen* (1834) brought the name back to public attention. In the United States, the short form of Clarence was Clare.

Claribel (G)
Fanciful name coined in the 16th century. Shakespeare called his Queen of Tunis in *The Tempest* Claribel, and Spenser addressed her in *Faerie Queene*.

Clarinda (G)
Fanciful name coined in the 16th century, it appears, like Claribel, in Spenser's *Faerie Queene* and was used as a Christian name in literary circles in the 17th and 18th centuries.

Clarissa (G)
Adapted by the novelist Samuel Richardson in the 18th century from the French Clarice, for his eponymous heroine Clarissa Harlow (1748). It means 'brightest'.

Clark (B)
American surname which became a Christian name in the 30s.

Claud (B)
Scottish version of the French Claude, which was adopted by the Hamilton family as a family Christian name. The Latin form was Claudius, meaning 'limping'.

Claude (B&G)
French, from Latin, used for both boys and girls.

Claudette (G)
French feminine diminutive of Claude, popularized here and in the United States by the film star Claudette Colbert.

Claudia (G)
Royal name of the Imperial Claudius family of Rome. A beautiful Claudia of Britain was described in verse by the Roman poet Martial, and Emperor Claudius sent his daughter Claudia to England to find out about Christianity.

Claudine (G)
French feminine diminutive of Claude popularized by the novels of Colette.

Clayton (B)
Surname which has become a Christian name. The short form is Clay.

Clea (G)
From Greek, meaning 'fame' or 'glory'. Lawrence Durrell's novel *Clea* is the final part of the *Alexandria Quartet*.

Clem (B)
Short form of Clement that dates from the 13th century. It has the association of 'mildness'.

Clemency (G)
From Latin 'clementia', meaning 'mildness'. Clementia was the earliest known form in the Middle Ages. Clemency was adopted by the Puritans as a 'virtue' name. It was a favourite in Edwardian times.

Clement (B)
From Latin, meaning 'mild' or 'merciful'. St Clement of Alexandria was a disciple of St Paul and is thought of as the patron saint of sailors. His name was revived as a Christian name at the end of the 19th century.

Clementine (G)
Originally from Latin, meaning 'mild', it was adopted from the German Klementine in the 18th century. Samuel Richardson has a Clementina in his play *Sir Charles Grandison* (1753) and it became an aristocratic name. In this century it is associated with the Hozier family. Clementine Hozier married Winston Churchill and her granddaughter Clementine was a bridesmaid at the royal wedding in 1981.

Cleo (G)
From Greek, meaning 'fame' or 'glory', a shortened form of Cleone and Cleopatra.

Cleone (G)
Greek, meaning 'fame' or 'glory'.

Cleopatra (G)
Greek, meaning 'fame of her father'.

Cliff (B)
Short form of Clifford, now a name in its own right.

Clifford (B)
A surname which became a Christian name for its aristocratic feel in the 1870s. It was probably an Anglo-Saxon
place name, describing a ford over a river.

Clio (G)
Greek, name of the muse of history.

Clive (B)
Name of a village in Shropshire first recorded in 1327 and
associated with a family of the region, a descendant of whom
was General Robert Clive, or Clive of India. His name was
first coined by the families who had connections with India
but by the 19th century it had become a common name.

Clodagh (G)
The name of a river in Tipperary, this Irish name was first
given by the Marquis of Waterford to his daughter.

Clothilda (G)
An Old Frankish name, dating from the sixth century, it
was a royal name meaning 'loud battle'. There has been
a fashion for medieval names in France recently and
Clothilde has been revived.

Clovis (B)
Ancient Frankish royal name, the name of Charlemagne's
son, derived from the Old German 'to fight'.

Cluny (G)
Scottish place name associated with clan MacPherson.

Colan (B)
Irish form of Colin, meaning 'a young hound' from the
Celtic 'cailean'.

Colette (G)
French, from Nicolette, its popularity in the 20th century
is due to the success of the French writer Sidonie Gabrielle
Claudine Colette, or Colette for short.

Nineties' names

The fashionable at the font

Smart parents favour the neo-nature – Sorrel, Storm, Cloudy, Coral, Windy, Savannah, Zephyr – as opposed to 60s' favourites, such as River, Willow and Sky.

They are Euro-chic and like medieval names such as Maximilian, Caspar, Clovis, Peregrine, Blanche and Cornelius. Classical Greek names – Dido, Phoebe, Artemisia, Pandora, Chloë, Theodore and Alexander – are more popular than the Roman Horace and Tarquin. Original Celtic – Gráinne, Ruaridh, Proinchéas – is preferred to the vernacular Grania, Rory and Frances. East-End names add street-cred – Alfie, Bert, Stan, Ned, Fred, Queenie, Ruby and Lily, though not Ron, Reggie or Terry, yet. Eastern names – Saffron, Kashmir, Uma – but not Western – Courtney, Cody, Page or Brooke. Mothers' maiden names are being used as second or third names.

The traditional at the font

Traditional parents prefer, but only marginally, Old Testament names – David, Samuel, Rebecca, Michael, Sarah, Hannah – to New Testament names – Thomas, James, Matthew and Luke. 80s' names – Sophie, Charlotte, Emily, Henry and William – are still popular and names that are unisex – Ashley, Ryan and Kerry. The traditional like to use a grandparent's or parent's Christian name as a second and third name to maintain a sense of family continuity.

Colin (B)
From the Celtic and Gaelic 'cailean', meaning 'young hound', Colin is found in the Middle Ages, but subsequently died out. It became a hereditary name of the Campbell family and from this association was adopted as a Christian name in the 19th century for its aristocratic feel.

Colleen (G)
Irish, literally with the meaning 'of girl'.

Colum (B)
Also written Colm, this Irish name has the meaning of 'dove' and is a very old name. Its most famous bearer was St Colum or St Columba who founded a monastery on Iona in the sixth century from which he converted Western Scotland to Christianity.

Columbus (B)
Surprise royal name coined by Lady Helen Windsor and Tim Taylor for their son Columbus George Donald Taylor. It is thought to be a reference to a London restaurant which was liked by the couple during their courting days.

Conal (B)
Irish name deriving from the Celtic, meaning 'high and mighty'.

Conan (B)
From Celtic, meaning 'intelligent', it was the name of a legendary seventh-century Irish chieftain Conan Moal, or Conan the Bald, and four dukes of Brittany. It was also the middle name of the creator of Sherlock Holmes, Sir Arthur Conan Doyle.

Conor (B)
Also written Connor, a popular Irish name meaning 'high desire' and associated with Irish legend and mythology.

Constance (G)
English form of the Latin 'constantia', meaning 'constancy', but spelt in Chaucer's and Shakespeare's time Custance.

Constancy (G)
One of the Puritan virtue names popular in the 17th century.

Queen Victoria's children

Nine children in 16 years, and what to call them? In all, thirty names were required to christen the children of Victoria and Albert.

Victoria's own christening had led to a family spat. Her father, Edward, Duke of Kent, wished her to be baptized Victoire Georgina Alexandrina Charlotte Augusta but the night before the christening his brother, Prince Regent, forbade three of the names on the grounds that Georgina, Charlotte and Augusta were the names of the English royal family and not to be used by the Kents. As for Victoire, it was French and therefore not suitable. At the christening Edward tentatively suggested Elizabeth, but it was quashed. A bewildered Archbishop of Canterbury asked, 'What then, shall I baptize this child?' The Prince Regent relented, 'Oh, give her the mother's name also then, but it cannot precede that of the Russian Emperor.' Hastily christened Alexandrina Victoria, the party quickly dispersed, but it was a humiliation which was never forgiven by the Kents.

Making up for the shortness of her own name, Victoria and Albert's first child, the Princess Royal, known as Pussy, was christened Victoria Adelaide Mary Louisa. The 'fine large boy' who followed in 1841 was named Albert Edward, after Victoria's husband and her father. A second daughter, a 'pretty and large baby who we think will be the beauty of the family' born in 1843, was baptized 'by the old English name' of Alice (Alice Maud Mary). Alfred Ernest Albert arrived in 1844, Helena Augusta Victoria in 1846, Louise Caroline Alberta (named after Albert's mother) in 1848. Arthur William Patrick Albert, born on the Duke of Wellington's 81st birthday and christened in his honour was followed by Leopold (after Victoria's uncle) George Duncan (reflecting her affection for Scotland) Albert, 'a jolly little fellow, but NO beauty'. Beatrice Mary Victoria Fedore, or Baby, 'the flower of the flock', brought up the rear and the nursery was complete.

Constantia (G)

The Latin for 'constancy', and a royal name of great distinction, given to the daughter of the first Christian Roman Emperor, Constantine the Great, and to the daughter of William the Conqueror. It was popular in England in the 19th century, ranking alongside Alice and Edith as faintly exotic names.

Constantine (B)

A name associated, perhaps surprisingly, with Scotland, and the name of four early Scottish kings. It is more importantly known as the name of the first Christian Emperor.

Cora (G)

From Greek, meaning 'girl'. It was popularized in the United States by James Fenimore Cooper in his book *The Last of the Mohicans* (1826).

Coral (G)

A late-19th-century jewel name sometimes used in this century.

Coralie (G)

From Greek, meaning 'little girl' and one of the names created after the French Revolution when there was a fashion for all things classical.

Cordelia (G)

In Welsh and Cornish legend Cordelia was the name of one of St Ursula's faithful companions. Shakespeare used it for the name of the equally loyal youngest daughter of King Lear.

Corin (B)

Masculine form of the Greek Cora.

Corinna (G)

A diminutive of the Greek Cora, meaning 'little girl'. A bestselling French novel, *Corinne*, brought it into general use at the start of the 19th century.

Cornelius (B)

From Latin, meaning 'war horn' and the name of a famous Roman family. It became popular in the Netherlands, where it was taken to the United States, becoming a favourite in the Vanderbilt family. It is tipped to become one of the surprise 'comebacks' of the 90s.

Cory (B)
An American name, derived from German, meaning 'the chosen one'.

Cosima (G)
From Greek, meaning 'order', the feminine form of Cosmo or Cosimo. It has been a favourite Italian name for many centuries. Cosima Liszt, who married Richard Wagner, was so-called because she was born on the shores of Lake Como in north Italy.

Cosimo (B)
From Greek, meaning 'order', which along with Cosmo, became aristocratic names of the Italian Renaissance. In Scotland, Cosimo has been used by the Gordon family since the 18th century.

Courtney (B&G)
French Norman, surname of the de Courtney family who came over with the Conqueror and settled in the West Country. From here, it went with the Pilgrim Fathers to the United States and has been a popular boy's and girl's name there for many centuries.

Craig (B)
Gaelic, from 'crag', meaning 'cliff'.

Cressida (G)
From Greek, meaning 'golden'. The story of Troilus and Cressida was retold in various ways by Boccaccio, Chaucer and Shakespeare.

Crispin (B)
From Latin, meaning 'curly-haired'. St Crispin was martyred in the third century and his name day, which Shakespeare made famous in *Henry V*, is 25 October.

Crystal (G)
Precious stone name popular in the United States.

Curran (B)
Celtic, meaning 'hero'.

A boy called Sue

It has been claimed by a psychologist that boys who are given what are thought of as girls' names such as Evelyn, Hilary and Jackie, grow up to be more rugged and macho than the Craigs, Scotts and Kevins of this world. Shirley Crabtree, also known as the wrestler Big Daddy, proves the rule. He was named after the heroine of his grandmother's favourite book, *Shirley* (1849), by Charlotte Brontë and spent a childhood living it down in the schoolyards of Halifax. But where fate had been cruel, nature was bountiful. By his own admission 'a big lad', at 16 he was in the professional ring and knocking the hell out of those wimpish Darrens, Freds and Berts.

Curtis (B)
French, meaning 'courteous'. A French surname which became a Christian name in the United States.

Cuthbert (B)
From Old English 'Cuthbeorht' with associations of 'famous' and 'bright', suggesting it was a noble name. St Cuthbert was the seventh-century Bishop of Lindisfarne and his name lived on in the north for hundreds of years. It was revived for its religious and English associations at the end of the 19th century.

Cynthia (G)
Greek, one of the names of Artemis, goddess of the moon, who was thought to dwell on Mt Cynthus in Greece. Elizabethan poets sometimes addressed their queen as Cynthia. It was in use in the seventh and 18th centuries and was very popular at the end of the 19th century for its classical associations.

Cyril (B)
From Greek 'kyrios', meaning 'lordly' and the name of two saints of Jerusalem and Alexandria. A later St Cyril took

Christianity to the Slavs and devised an alphabet for them, which became known as the Cyrillic. His name was revived in England in the late 19th century.

Cyrus (B)

From Persian, 'kuru' meaning 'throne'. Cyrus the Great was King of Persia and his name appears in the Old Testament. It remains a favourite Israeli name.

D

Dagmar (G)
Scandinavian, meaning 'glorious days'.

Dahlia (G)
Flower name which came into use at the end of the 19th century. Bertie Wooster's favourite aunt was called Dahlia.

Dai (B)
Welsh, a shortened form of Dafydd or David.

Daisy (G)
One of the flower names of the last 200 years, from the Anglo-Saxon, meaning 'day's eye', referring to the golden centre and the petals that close at dusk.

Dale (B)
From the Yorkshire name for 'valley'. In the United States it is used as a girl's name. It has been very popular in Scotland since the 80s.

Damian (B)
From Greek, meaning 'to tame', it appears in the New Testament as the name of one of a pair of brothers martyred in Syria in the fourth century. Popular in the Middle Ages and revived in the 19th century when there was a fashion for classical names.

Damon (B)
From Greek, meaning 'to tame'.

Dana (G)
Celtic goddess of fertility whose name has survived in Ireland.

Daniel (B)
From Hebrew, meaning 'God is judge' and one of the great Old Testament names. The name has been in use since the

Middle Ages, even undergoing a revival in the last 15 years. It is now in the top ten list of boys' names.

Daniella (G)
Italian feminine form of Daniel which, with the French version Danielle, has become popular in the last 30 years. They both have the associated meaning of 'god is judge'.

Daphne (G)
From Greek, meaning 'bay-tree' or 'laurel'. In Greek legend Daphne was a nymph who turned into a laurel tree to protect herself from Apollo's attentions. The name came into use at the turn of the century when there was a fashion for classical Greek and Roman names.

Darcy (B&G)
A branch of the D'Areci family who came over from Normandy at the time of the Conquest and settled in Ireland. In the last century their name was adopted as a Christian name. Fitzwilliam Darcy was the name of Elizabeth Bennet's admirer in *Pride and Prejudice*. The ballerina Darcy Bussell has shown that it works as well for girls as boys.

Daria (G)
Greek feminine form of the Persian Darius, meaning 'regal'.

Darius (B)
Greek form of the Persian 'dara', meaning 'king'. Darius the Great assumed the title when he became ruler of Persia in 521 BC.

Darrell (B)
Norman aristocratic surname which came into use as a Christian name in the present century. An alternative spelling is Daryl.

Darren (B)
From Irish, meaning 'great'. Since the 70s it has been in the top 40 boys' names in Scotland.

David (B)
Hebrew, meaning 'darling'. In the Old Testament David slew Goliath and became the second King of Israel. Despite being in use in England for less than a century, it has been popular in Wales in one form or another for nearly 1,400

A girl called India

China has been and gone, Asia may be yet to come, but it looks like India is here to stay as a Christian name. It was first given to the second daughter of Lady Pamela Mountbatten and David Hicks born in 1967 and named in honour of her grandmother, Lady Edwina Mountbatten, whose great love of India extended well beyond her Vice-Reineship of 1947.

Lady India Hicks was a bridesmaid at the wedding of the Prince of Wales and Lady Diana Spencer in 1981 and as a result there has been a flurry of little Indias at the registry offices and christening fonts all over the globe. Reported to be one of the commonest Christian names for little girls in the London Borough of Kensington and Chelsea, even celebrities have not been immune: Jeff Banks has a daughter called India, as does Catherine Oxenburg. Meanwhile in Australia, Mrs Joanne Abadee of Pymble, Sydney chose the name for her daughter, born 8 October 1991. She told a reporter from the *Sydney Morning Herald*: 'She has colic, so we call her Windy Indy.'

---

years through the association with St David, patron saint of Wales. In Scotland too it has strong roots, belonging to kings, nobles and common men in equal measure. Since 1958 it has been the name favoured by Scottish parents above all others.

Davida (G)
Scottish feminine form of David, with the association of 'darling' dating from the 17th century. A variation is Davina.

Dawn (G)
Translation of the Latin 'aurora', meaning 'dawn', it first

appeared as a name in the United States at the end of the 19th century.

Dean (B)
American, with the association of the Anglo-Saxon word for 'valley'.

Deanna (G)
American form of Diana, popularized in the 30s by the young film actress, Deanna Durbin.

Deborah (G)
From Hebrew, meaning 'a bee'. The song of Deborah the prophetess is one of the oldest poems in the Old Testament. The Puritans, who loved Old Testament names, revived it in the 17th century and the poet John Milton called his daughter Deborah.

Debra (G)
American spelling of Deborah.

Deirdre (G)
Celtic name, which appears in Old Irish as 'Derdriu', meaning 'the raging one', and in Gaelic as 'Deoirid', meaning 'the broken-hearted one'. It was popularized by Irish and Scots poets and novelists at the start of the 20th century.

Delia (G)
From Greek, meaning 'circle' or 'moon', and taken from the name of the island of Delos in the Aegean which was reputedly the birthplace of Artemis and Apollo. It was a favourite of pastoral poets of the 17th and 18th centuries who were fond of pretty classical names and was revived again, for general use, at the end of the 19th century when classical names were in vogue.

Delilah (G)
Hebrew, with the meaning 'delight'. It has been popular for its Old Testament associations in the Southern states of America.

Delphine (G)
From Greek, meaning 'larkspur'.

Demelza (G)
Cornish place name.

Demetria (G)
Greek, meaning 'of mother earth'.

Denis (B)
French form of the Greek name Dionysos, meaning 'divine one of Nysa' in reference to his role in Greek mythology as the god of wine, Nysa being famous for its vineyards. St Dionysius, later called St Denis, is the patron saint of France and his name was brought to England – as Dionis – at the end of the 12th century. It was revived at the end of the 19th century for its medieval feel and was immensely popular in the 20s and 30s.

Denise (G)
French feminine form of Denis, with the associated meaning of 'divine one of Nysa' from its Greek origin as the name of the god of wine and festivals. Denise has been in frequent use since the 50s.

Dennis (B)
Irish form of the French Denis.

Denys (B)
Welsh form of the French Denis.

Denzil (B)
Old Cornish, with the meaning 'of high stronghold' and originally a place name that was first adopted as a surname by the landowning family of the region, and subsequently used as a Christian name. Denzil Holles was a famous Cornish MP of the 17th century. An alternative spelling is Denzell.

Derek (B)
Flemish form of the Greek Theodoric, meaning 'gift of God'. It was introduced to England in the 15th century as Deryk or Dederick, but fell into disuse for many centuries. The present century has seen a handsome revival.

Derick (B)
Alternative spelling of Derek, reminiscent of the early Flemish Deryck which first arrived in England in the 15th century.

Dermot (B)
From Old Irish 'Diarmuit', meaning 'free man'. Dermot

McMurrough was King of Leinster in the 12th century and his name has long been popular in Tipperary and Limerick.

Deryck (B)
Original Flemish form of Derek, introduced to England in the 15th century.

Desirée (G)
French, meaning 'desired' and sometimes used in this century for its continental feel. Desiderata was an English medieval form of the same name.

Desmond (B)
From Irish 'deas munster', describing those who came from South Munster. It came into use as a Christian name in England from the end of the 19th century.

Dewi (B)
Old Welsh name for St David, the sixth-century patron saint of Wales. In later centuries St David was known as Dafydd. Dewi seems to have been a Celtic name and probably associated with royalty, since it was also the name of two early Scottish kings.

Dexter (B)
A surname which has come into used as a Christian name in the present century.

Diana (G)
In Roman mythology Diana was both moon goddess and huntress, like her Greek counterpart, Artemis. The name came to England from France in the 16th century and quickly became a favourite literary name for its classical associations. It has been in general use from the 18th century.

Diane (G)
French name for the goddess Diana which was popularized by Diane de Poitiers, a renowned and celebrated 16th-century beauty. Today it is quite a rare Christian name, Diana being far more usual.

Diarmuit (B)
Old Irish, meaning 'free man'. In Irish legend Diarmuit eloped with Gráinne (or Grania), the Queen of Tara. The name has always been a favourite name in Tipperary and Limerick. The English form is Dermot.

Dick (B)
Short form of Richard in use since the Middle Ages when it was created as a rhyming nickname for Rick. It became so popular that it was used, like Jack, to mean an ordinary man. Tom, Dick and Harry were the quintessential solid Englishmen.

Dickon (B&G)
Old English diminutive of Dick which was popularized by Frances Hodgson Burnett's *The Secret Garden* (1911).

Dido (G)
Greek, name of the legendary Queen of Carthage.

Digby (B)
A surname which was adopted as a Christian name in the 19th century.

Diggory (B)
Derived from the French, meaning 'strayed' or 'lost'; a popular name in Cornwall for many centuries.

Dilys (G)
Welsh, meaning 'sincere' or 'genuine'. It came into English usage at the end of the last century when there was a fashion for Welsh names.

Dinah (G)
Hebrew, meaning 'judged'. In the Old Testament, Dinah was the daughter of Jacob and Leah. It was revived for its biblical associations by the Puritans in the 17th century and was taken to the United States where it became popular in the South.

Dionne (G)
Modern American version of the medieval Dionysia, a girl's name associated with the Greek god of wine and festivals.

Dirk (B)
Dutch form of Derek, meaning 'gift of God'.

Dodie (G)
Short form of Dorothy, it is also occasionally used for Josephine.

Cornish names

The Cornish were originally Celtic people, driven out of
Britain by the invading Anglo-Saxons in the sixth century. They settled, like the Welsh, Manx and Scots, in
the western extremities of the British Isles. The Cornish,
Welsh and Bretons shared a similar language and culture
and this was reflected in their names. Morwenna is, for
example, a Cornish name but has the common Celtic
'myr' or 'mor' meaning 'sea' and is related to the Welsh
'morwang' meaning 'wave of the sea', while Jenifer
is the Cornish form of the Welsh Gwenhwyver or
Guenevere. A remarkably adventurous people, it has
recently been shown that the Cornish had close links
with the Phoenicians of North Africa some 2,000 years
ago which may go some way to explain the popularity
of the name Hannibal over many centuries in Cornwall.

There has been a revival of interest in Cornish names
in recent years and many are suitable, if not for first
names, then certainly for second or third names.

Boys

Austol   Breton saint who gave his name to St Austell

Cador   Name of a legendary ruler of Cornwall, meaning 'warrior'

Carasek   Name of a legendary Duke of Cornwall and
famous first-century chieftain, meaning 'amiable'.
A variation is Caradok

Caswyn   Old Cornish, meaning 'fair battle'

Colan   Name of a Celtic saint who gave his name to
Colan near Newquay, and in use up to the 17th century

Conan   Name of a semi-historcial Cornish king

Cornelly   Cornish form of Cornelius

Costetyn   Cornish form of Constantine

Davy   Cornish and Devonian form of David which
dates from the 17th century

Gawen Cornish form of Gawain, the name of King Arthur's most illustrious knight

Gerens Cornish form of Geraint and the name of a king of Cornwall

Kenal Old Cornish, meaning 'generous chief'

Kenwyn Old Cornish, meaning 'splendid chief'

Kevern Name of a Cornish saint who gave his name to St Keverne

Manuel Spanish form of Emanuel which was very popular in Cornwall before the 18th century

Myghal Old Cornish form of Michael, pronounced Ma-hail

Pasco Cornish form of Pascal in use until the 18th century and traditionally given to boys born at Eastertime

Perran Name of one of the two patron saints of Cornwall.

Petrok Name of one of the two patron saints of Cornwall who gave his name to Padstow (Petrok's stow)

Samson Old Testament name which has been in use in Cornwall for many centuries

Trystan Cornish form of Tristan, the hero of the medieval romance

Girls

Angelet Cornish form of the French Angel

Barenwyn Old Cornish, meaning 'fair branch'

Columba Cornish feminine form of Colum or Colm

Cordelia From the Old Welsh Cordula and a name found in early parish registers

Demelza Cornish place name popularized by Winston Graham's Poldark novels

Elestren Cornish, meaning 'iris'

Eselt   Old Cornish form of Iseult

Jenifer   Cornwall's most popular export! It is the Cornish form of the Welsh Gwenhwyver or Norman Guinevere and has become one of the classic names of the 20th century. The English spelling is Jennifer

Mariot   Cornish form of Miriam which was in use until the 18th century

Melloney   Cornish form of Melanie which has been in use since the 17th century

Neraud   Cornish name recorded in 1296, meaning 'little one of the sea'

Morvoren   Cornish meaning 'mermaid'

Tamsyn   Medieval feminine form of Thomas which was very popular in Cornwall

---

Dolly (G)
Pet form of Dorothy which came into use at the start of the 18th century. In the present century it has often been given as a name in its own right.

Dolores (G)
Spanish name which has come into English usage in the last 50 years from the United States. In Spain it is always given as a Christian name in association with Maria. It means 'sorrows'. Maria de los Dolores means 'Mary of the Sorrows'.

Dominic (B)
From Latin, 'dies dominica', or 'day of the Lord', and traditionally given to boys born on a Sunday. Its use was discouraged after the Protestant Reformation in this country, although it continued to be used by Catholic families. In this century there has been a revival among parents of all denominations.

Dominique (G)

French, meaning 'of the Lord' and adopted into English since the 50s for its Gallic feel.

Dónal (B)

Irish form of the Scottish Donald.

Donald (B)

Royal Scottish name, born by six Scottish kings. The original Gaelic is 'Domhnall' (pronounced Daw-nal).

Donna (G)

Italian title for 'lady'. It has only been used as a Christian name in this century.

Donovan (B)

Irish surname which has become a Christian name, meaning 'dark brown', a description of the colour of someone's hair or eyes.

Dora (G)

Originally a shortened form of Theodora or Dorothea, Dora became a name in its own right in the 19th century. Its meaning comes from the Greek 'doron', meaning 'gift'.

Dorabella (G)

Theatrical 18th-century name popularized by Mozart in his opera *Così Fan Tutte* (1790). Another 18th-century fanciful name is Doralinda.

Doreen (G)

English form of the Irish Celtic 'Doirean', meaning 'sullen'. Its use in England dates from the publication of a popular novel by Edna Lyall called *Doreen* (1894).

Dorian (B)

Greek, meaning 'of the sea'.

Dorinda (G)

Theatrical 18th-century name that was coined for George Farquhar's *The Beaux Stratagem* (1707).

Doris (G)

From Greek, meaning 'gift'. In Greek mythology Doris was the daughter of Oceanus and the mother of the sea-nymphs or nereids. It came into use in England at the end of the 19th century when classical names were popular.

Dorothea (G)
From Greek, meaning 'gift of God' and introduced in the 18th century as a variation of Dorothy. The most famous Dorothea of all must be George Eliot's Dorothea Brooke in her novel *Middlemarch*.

Dorothy (G)
From Greek, meaning 'gift of God'. Very popular in the 16th and 17th centuries, the name then fell out of fashion to be revived for its classical associations at the end of the 19th century.

Dougal (B)
From Old Irish 'dubgall', meaning 'dark stranger' and initially used by the Irish to describe the dark-haired Danes.

Douglas (B)
From Gaelic 'dubhglas', meaning 'dark water', and initially a clan name. Sir James Douglas was a companion of Robert the Bruce. By the 16th century it had become popular south of the border and in Scotland in the 19th century for its aristocratic associations.

Doyle (B)
Modern Irish, meaning 'dark stranger'.

Drina (G)
Pet form of Alexandrina and the name by which Queen Victoria was known as a child.

Drusilla (G)
Latin, meaning 'of the family of Drusus'. It was a Roman patrician name, used by the Livian family, Livia Drusilla being the second wife of the great Emperor Augustus. However, the name also appears in the New Testament and it was this which caused it to be favoured by the Puritans.

Dudley (B)
Family surname of the earls of Leicester, the most famous of whom was Robert Dudley, favourite of Queen Elizabeth I. The name came into use in the 19th century for its aristocratic feel.

Duff (B)
From Gaelic, meaning 'black-haired'.

Dulce (G)
Latin, pronounced Dul-che, meaning 'sweet'.

Dulcia (G)
Latin, pronounced Dul-chia, meaning 'sweet'.

Dulcie (G)
English form of Dulcia, meaning 'sweet'.

Dulcinea (G)
Spanish, meaning 'sweet and beautiful' and the name chosen by Don Quixote for his pretty companion in Cervantes' 17th-century masterpiece *Don Quixote*.

Duncan (B)
From Gaelic 'donn chadh' and Irish 'donn cean', meaning 'brown warrior'. Duncan was the name of two early Scottish kings, one of whom was murdered by Macbeth. It became a popular name south of the border in the 19th century for its royal Scottish associations.

Dunstan (B)
Old English, with association of 'hill' and 'stone'. St Dunstan was Archbishop of Canterbury in the tenth century and his name was revived and brought into use for its religious associations at the end of the 19th century.

Dwayne (B)
Irish surname, meaning 'the singer'. An alternative spelling is Duane.

Dwight (B)
English surname used first as a Christian name in New England.

Dylan (B)
Welsh, meaning 'son of the wave' and pronounced Dulan. Bob Dylan, who was born Robert Zimmerman, took his name from the poet Dylan Thomas.

E

Eamon (B)
Irish form of Edmund, with the association of 'prosperity'.

Eartha (G)
Traditionally the name given to the third child in the Southern states of America if the first two had been lost. Named after the Mother Earth, the safety of the child was ensured.

Eben (B)
Hebrew, meaning 'stone'.

Ebony (G)
Greek, meaning 'a dark wood'. It can also be spelt Ebonee.

Edgar (B)
Anglo-Saxon, meaning 'prosperous by the spear'. It was a royal name and King Edgar, who was the first king of a united England, was a great grandson of Alfred the Great. His name was revived by Scott in his novel *The Bride of Lammermoor* (1819) and became a Victorian favourite.

Edith (G)
Anglo-Saxon, meaning 'prosperous in war'. It was a royal name, the name of two English queens and several Saxon princesses. A variation was Editha. The name was revived in the 19th century for its historical feel.

Edmond (B)
Norman spelling of Old English Edmund.

Edmund (B)
Old English, with the meaning of 'guardian of prosperity'. The name of two English kings and two early English saints, it was in constant use until the end of the Middle Ages. It was revived in the 19th century for its historical and royal feel.

Edna (G)

Probably of Hebrew origin, meaning 'rejuvenation', Edna appears in the Old Testament as the mother of Sarah. Its popularity in Ireland may be due to an old Anglo-Saxon name, Edana.

Edward (B)

Anglo-Saxon, with the meaning of 'guardian of prosperity'. A royal name for over 1,000 years, it is one of the few names which passed from English into other European languages. The French Edouard, German Eduard, Italian Eduardo and Portuguese Duarte all owe their origins to the English Edward.

Edwin (B)

Anglo-Saxon, with the meaning of 'friend of prosperity'. St Edwine was the first Christian king of Northumberland and gave his name to Edinburgh, or Edwin's Burgh. It was revived in the 18th century for its historical associations.

Edwina (G)

Feminine form of Edwin, meaning 'friend of prosperity'. It came back into use at the end of the 19th century for its medieval feel.

Edwy (B)

Anglo-Saxon, with the meaning 'beloved of prosperity'.

Effie (G)

Scottish pet form of Euphemia, meaning 'pleasant speech'. Another variation is Phemie, pronounced 'fay-me'. Both names have been rooted in Scottish culture and literature for centuries.

Eibhlín (G)

Irish, pronounced 'eye-leen' or 'ev-leen' depending on the part of Ireland you find yourself. The English form is Eileen.

Eileen (G)

English form of Irish Eibhlín, meaning 'pleasant'. It became popular in England at the the end of the 19th century when there was a great deal of interest in Irish, Welsh and Scottish names.

Eilidh (G)
Scots Gaelic form of Helen, which is currently in the list of top 50 girls' names in Scotland.

Eiluned (G)
Welsh, meaning 'idol' and pronounced Eli-ned. An alternative spelling is Eluned.

Eirene (G)
Greek, meaning 'peace', originally spelt Irene.

Elain (G)
Welsh, meaning 'fawn' or 'young hind'.

Elaine (G)
Old French form of Helena, meaning 'the bright one'. Elaine or Elain were names in their own right in the ancient Celtic languages of France and Britain, probably meaning 'fawn' or 'young hind', since the name occurs in Arthurian legend. The poet Tennyson revived interest in the name in the 19th century.

Eldred (B)
From Anglo-Saxon, meaning 'noble counsel'.

Eleanor (G)
Medieval variation of Helen, meaning 'the bright one'. The name was brought to England by Eleanor (whose name was spelt in the Provençal fashion Alienor) of Aquitaine, who married Henry II. It was revived in the 19th century when there was a particular interest in medieval names, in this form and also spelt Elinor.

Eleanora (G)
Italian form of Eleanor. The name was sometimes used in England in the 19th century when there was a fashion for Italian names.

Electra (G)
From Greek, meaning 'amber'.

Elena (G)
Italian and Spanish form of Helen, meaning 'bright one'.

Elfreda (G)
From Old English, meaning 'elf-strength'. A royal Saxon

name, like Emma, it did not survive the Norman Conquest, but was revived in the 19th century.

Eli (B)
From Hebrew, meaning 'height' and the name of the priest who brought up Samuel. The Puritans revived the name in the 17th century and took it to the United States where it has remained popular.

Elias (B)
From Hebrew, meaning 'Jehovah is God'.

Elinor (G)
17th-century spelling of Eleanor, replaced in the 19th century by Eleanor. Elinor Dashwood appears in Jane Austen's *Sense and Sensibility*.

Elisabeth (G)
French form of Elizabeth, meaning 'oath of God'.

Elise (G)
French short form of Elizabeth.

Elisheba (G)
Hebrew, meaning 'oath of God'. Elizabeth comes from the Latin translation of the name, but Elisheba is close to the Hebrew original. In the Old Testament, Elisheba, who lived in 1200 BC, was Aaron's wife.

Elissa (G)
Greek, another name for Dido, daughter of Belus of Tyre who became Queen of Carthage.

Eliza (G)
Short form of Elizabeth which was first used as a poetic address to Queen Elizabeth I. It became a name in its own right in the 18th and 19th centuries. In the present century it is associated with George Bernard Shaw's Eliza Doolittle.

Elizabeth (G)
From Hebrew, meaning 'oath of God'. Elizabetha was the Latin form of the name Elisheba. It passed initially into French as Isabel and arrived in England in the 15th century in the form Elizabeth, becoming, in the next century, an established royal name. By 1600, one in five girls were

christened Elizabeth, a figure which did not change for 200 years. Although its popularity has dipped slightly, it remains one of the classic names for all seasons and all centuries.

Ella (G)
From Old German, meaning 'all'. It was introduced to England by the Normans and was in common use until Elizabethan times. The Pre-Raphaelites liked it for its medieval feel.

Elle (G)
Short form of Eleanor, popularized in late 80s and 90s by the Australian supermodel Elle Macpherson. She shortened her name when she became the house-model for *Elle* magazine in 1981. Tipped as a name for the 90s.

Ellen (G)
From Greek, meaning 'the bright one'. It was the earliest form of Helen in England, along with Eleanor, and has always been a particular favourite in Scotland. Sir Walter Scott chose it for the heroine of his poem 'The Lady of the Lake' (1810) and it became a favourite Victorian name.

Ellis (G)
Diminutive of Eleanor and, in Ireland, of Ella.

Ellis (B)
English version of Elias or Elijah, with its Hebrew meaning 'Jehovah is God'.

Eloïse (G)
From Old French Heloïse, meaning 'famous woman warrior'.

Elroy (B)
French, meaning 'belonging to the king'. It seems to have been a surname in the 18th century, in use among the French settlers of Louisiana.

Elsa (G)
From Old German, meaning 'noble maiden'. The Scottish form is Ailsa.

Aristocratic surnames as Christian names

In the 20th century we have become so accustomed to the use of names such as Dudley, Howard, Clifford, Russell, Cameron and Graham as Christian names that it comes as something of a surprise to realize that they form a small catalogue of the names of the great landed families of England and Scotland, and were adopted for general use as Christian names in the 19th century.

In fact, the aristocracy had been preserving family names, particularly mother's maiden names, by using them as Christian names since the 16th century. It was a way of passing on rights to land and family fortunes. Lord Guildford Dudley, husband of Lady Jane Grey, received his mother's maiden name Guildford, as his Christian name and the first Winston Churchill, born 1620, was named after his mother Sarah Winston, daughter of Sir Henry Winston of Standish in Gloucester. Two centuries later, the poet Percy Bysshe Shelley could trace his Christian name back to the Percys, earls and subsequently dukes of Northumberland since the fourteenth century.

Surnames which came into use as Christian names in the 19th century for their aristocratic flavour:

Cameron	Howard	Sidney
Cecil	Keith	Stanley
Clarence	Montague	Stewart
Dudley	Mortimer	Stuart
Graham	Neville	Wallace
Hamilton	Percy	
Herbert	Russell	

Elspeth (G)
Scottish form of Elizabeth.

Elton (B)
Surname turned Christian name coined by Elton John, whose original name was Reg Dwight.

Elvira (G)
Spanish, although it originally came from Old German and was brought to Spain by the Goths, with the meaning 'elf-counsel'. There have been two notable fictional Elviras: Mozart's lady of virtue in his opera *Don Giovanni* and the heroine of Waldemar Bergendahl's classic 1967 film *Elvira Madigan*.

Elvis (B)
Scandinavian, meaning 'all-wise'.

Elwyn (G)
Welsh, meaning 'fair-browed'.

Elysia (G)
From Greek, meaning 'paradise'.

Em (G)
Short form of Emma dating from the 18th century.

Emanuel (B)
From Hebrew, meaning 'God with us', and the name given to the Messiah. The Greeks shortened the name to Manuel and it spread through Spain and Portugal. Perhaps because of the seafaring links, it was a popular name in Cornwall in the 16th and 17th centuries.

Emelie (G)
Chaucer's spelling of Emily in 'The Knight's Tale' brought the name to attention in the 15th century.

Emerald (G)
Jewel-name made popular in the 20s by Maude Burke who changed her name to Emerald when she married Sir Bache Cunard. The Spanish form, which is much older, is Esmeralda.

Emily (G)
From Italian, meaning 'winning'. An Emilia appeared in Boccaccio's *Decameron* and Geoffrey Chaucer, seeing the

name, introduced it into the English language as Emelie in his *Canterbury Tales*. Not until the 18th century did the name properly establish itself. George II's daughter was christened Amelia, but known as Emily. It became a classic Victorian name and was revived in the 80s.

Emlyn (B)
Welsh, a place name in Dyfed.

Emma (G)
From Old German, meaning 'whole' and a medieval royal name. Emma, daughter of the Duke of Normandy, married into the Saxon royal family. The name came back into fashion in the 18th century and was put firmly on the map by Jane Austen's novel, *Emma* (1816). It has seen a steady revival since the 50s and has been in the top ten names for girls since 1985. In Scotland it has held first position since 1990.

Emmanuelle (G)
French feminine form of Emanuel, meaning 'God with us'.

Emmeline (G)
From Old German, meaning 'little Emma', introduced by the Normans.

Ena (G)
English form of the Irish Aine or Aithne. Queen Victoria's granddaughter was christened Victoria Eugenie, but known as Ena. She married Alfonso of Spain and was known as Princess Ena, a name which has stayed in the Spanish royal family.

Enid (G)
English form of Welsh 'Eanid', meaning 'life' or 'soul'. Eanid seems to be a very ancient Celtic name and it appears in many medieval legends, including stories of King Arthur and the Knights of the Round Table. The English form Enid dates from the popularity of Tennyson's poem 'Geraint and Enid' (1859).

Enoch (B)
Hebrew, meaning 'dedication'. Enoch, in the Old Testament is a descendant of Adam. A similar name Enog is Old Welsh.

Names to get rich with

Each year the *Sunday Times* publishes a list of Britain's wealthiest 500 people. While the balance between inherited wealth and self-made wealth shifts – until 1994, the list was split half and half between the two, but now old wealth accounts for less than a third of the 500 – the Christian names of Britain's wealthiest remain fairly static. It seems that if you wish to make money it is an advantage to have a simple, straightforward name and preferably one which does not mark you out from your peer group. Just 15 names account for over half of the 360 men and women who make up the 'new-wealth' category.

They are:

John (36), David (28), Peter (24), Michael (22), Robert (15), Paul (10), Richard (9), Thomas (8), Alan (8), Nigel (7), George (6), Tony (6), William (6), Ian (6), and Anthony (6).

Since the majority of Britain's wealthiest were born before the 50s, their names reflect the fashions of the time. Names such as Simon, Mark, Matthew and Daniel occur in only one or two instances since they were given as popular Christian names in the 60s and 70s.

A tip for parents wishing their children to appear on the *Sunday Times* list of Britain's wealthiest in 2040: call them David, Matthew, Thomas, James, Christopher, Michael, Jamie, Luke, Callum, Alexander, Rebecca, Sarah, Jessica, Lauren, Emma, Hannah, Catherine, Chloë, Sophie or Amy, that is, the most popular first names in Britain today.

Eppie (G)
Scottish shortened form of Euphemia, meaning 'pleasant speech'. St Euphemia was an early Christian whom the lions refused to devour, and her name became very popular in Scotland. One of James Boswell's daughters was known as Eppie.

Erasma (G)
From Greek, meaning 'desired' or 'beloved'.

Erasmus (G)
From Greek, meaning 'desired' or 'beloved.

Eric (B)
From Old Norse, meaning 'ruler'. It was a favourite Viking name and spread with their conquests of Northern Europe for its royal associations. Nearly 1,000 years later it was revived as a Victorian name as a result of Rider Haggard's Norse romance *Eric Brighteyes* and was popular in the 20s and 30s.

Erica (G)
A feminine form of Eric that came into use at the end of the last century. Erica is also the botanical name for 'heather', which contributed to its success as a flower or plant name.

Erik (B)
Modern Scandinavian form of Eric. Six Danish kings and 14 Swedish ones have borne the name.

Erinna (G)
From Irish, meaning 'peace'.

Ernest (B)
From Old German, meaning 'vigour'. Ernst was a popular aristocratic name in Germany from the tenth century but was hardly known in England until the marriage of Queen Victoria and Albert of Saxe-Coburg, Ernst or Ernest being a family name of the Saxe-Coburg family which was bestowed on their second child. The name was immortalized by Oscar Wilde in *The Importance of Being Earnest*.

Ernestine (G)
French feminine form of Ernest, sometimes found in the 19th century.

Errol (B)
English surname which came into use as a Christian name in the 19th century following the publication of Frances Hodgson Burnett's *Little Lord Fauntleroy*, whose hero is Cedric Errol.

Erskine (B)
Scottish family name which is sometimes used as a Christian name.

Erwin (B)
From Anglo-Saxon, meaning 'the sea's friend'.

Esha (G)
Hindu, meaning 'desire'.

Esme (B)
Scottish version of French Esmé, meaning 'beloved'. It was first given as a name in the family of the dukes of Lennox in the 17th century.

Esmé (G)
Also spelt Esmée, from Old French, meaning 'beloved'.

Esmeralda (G)
Spanish, meaning 'emerald', used in Spain from the 16th century.

Esmond (B)
Among the oldest English names still in use, Esmond appears in Anglo-Saxon records as 'Estmund', meaning 'protection'. It became popular in the 19th century for its old English feel.

Estelle (G)
French version of the Latin stella, meaning 'star'.

Esther (G)
Persian, meaning 'star'. Esther's real name was Hadassah, but she was captured and made the wife of the Persian King Ahasuerus who gave her the new name of Esther. The Book of Esther forms part of the Old Testament and the name was adopted by the Puritans in the 17th century.

Estrella (G)
Spanish, meaning 'star'.

Ethel (G)
From Anglo-Saxon, meaning 'noble' and a royal name associated with Northumbrian kings. It was revived in the 19th century for its historic associations.

Ethelia (G)
St Etheldred was Queen of Northumbria in the seventh century and became founder and abbess of a convent at Ely. Audrey was one descendant of her name, and Ethelia another. A pretty alternative to Ethel.

Etta (G)
From German, meaning 'happy' or 'blessed' and pronounced Yet-ta.

Euan (B)
Irish form of Ewan, from Celtic 'eoghain', meaning 'youth'. In the last 20 years, it has replaced the traditional spelling Ewan in Scotland in popularity.

Eugene (B)
From Greek, meaning 'well-born' or 'born lucky', it came into use in England in the 18th century through its association with Prince Eugène of Savoy who fought with the Duke of Marlborough against Louis XIV of France. The popularity of the name in the United States produced the short form Gene.

Eugenie (G)
French from Greek, meaning 'nobility' or 'excellence'. Eugenia was recorded in England in the Middle Ages, but it was the popularity of Empress Eugénie of France in the 19th century that created a fashion for her name.

Eustace (B)
Revived by the Victorians for its aristocratic feel, Eustace came originally from Greek, with the meaning 'plentiful harvest', and had been brought over to England by the Normans.

Eva (G)
Latin version of Eve, meaning 'life'.

Evan (B)
Welsh form of John dating from the 16th century and pronounced 'Ifan'.

Evangeline (G)
Invented by Longfellow for his narrative poem 'Evangeline' written in 1847, it became quite a common name in the United States.

Eve (G)
From Hebrew, meaning 'life', so-called according to the Book of Genesis 'because she was the mother of all things'. Her name was not used by the Jews, but appeared in its Latin form, Eva, here in the 12th century.

Evelina (G)
Latin form of the Old French girls' name Aveline, meaning 'hazelnut'. It was revived by the novelist Fanny Burney for the heroine of her popular novel *Evelina* in 1778.

Evelyn (G)
From the Old French name Aveline, meaning 'hazelnut' which was the ancient fruit of wisdom. It was a name given to girls of Norman nobility and was brought to England with the Normans.

Evelyn (B)
From Old French, meaning 'hazelnut', Evelyn became a surname in the Middle Ages and was first given as a Christian name to Evelyn Pierrepont, first Duke of Kingston in 1665. It came into general use in the 19th century for its aristocratic associations.

Ewan (B)
Scottish and Irish name from the Celtic 'eoghain', meaning 'youth', it is also related to the Welsh Owen.

Ezra (B)
Hebrew, meaning 'help', it was a popular name for its biblical association with the Puritans and went with them to the United States.

F

Fabia (G)

Latin form of the French Fabienne. St Fabian was an early saint and pope who came from a powerful Roman family called the Fabii. The Italian form is Fabiola.

Faine (G)

From Anglo-Saxon, meaning 'joyful'.

Faith (G)

A name coined for its literal meaning by the Puritans in the 17th century. It has survived nicely into the present century.

Fanny (G)

Pet form of Frances which came into use in the 19th century. An older pet form was Franny. Frances Burney, known as Fanny, was lady-in-waiting to Queen Charlotte and made her name writing romantic novels with spirited heroines.

Farquhar (B)

From the Gaelic Fearchar, meaning 'friendly'. It was the name of an early Scottish king and has been in use over many centuries in the Highlands.

Fay (G)

Also spelt Faye. A variation of Faith which was created in the 19th century.

Feargus (B)

Irish Celtic 'ver gusti', meaning 'man of strength'. The Scottish Gaelic version is Fearghas and the Pictish form is Forcus. This ancient name was the name of ten Celtic saints and several legendary heroes. Feargus Mac Erca led the Gaels from Ireland to Scotland in the fifth century. In the English spelling Fergus, it has become one of the most popular Celtic names in general use.

Fedora (G)
Italian feminine form of the Russian name Fyodor, which means 'gift of God'.

Felice (G)
English spelling of the medieval French girls' name Felise meaning 'happy'.

Felicia (G)
Latin, the feminine form of Felix meaning 'happy'.

Felicity (G)
From Latin, meaning 'happiness'. In Roman mythology she was the patron saint of good luck and her name was also borne by a Carthaginian saint. The Puritans loved biblical names and Felicity came into use for the first time in England in the 17th century.

Felix (B)
From Latin, meaning 'happy'. St Felix of East Anglia gave his name to Felixstowe. It was revived at the end of the 19th century when classical names were popular.

Fenella (G)
English form of the Gaelic Fionnghuala, meaning 'white shoulders'. Sir Walter Scott's *Peveril of the Peak* (1822) featured a Fenella.

Ferdinand (B)
Originally from Old German, with associations of journey and risk, it was carried to Spain by the Goths and became a royal name. In the 16th century the Italian form Ferdinando was used as a Christian name by the English nobility.

Fergal (B)
Irish, meaning 'man of strength'. St Fergal was an eighth-century Irish saint. The Irish Gaelic form is Fearghal.

Fergus (B)
English form of the Irish Feargus, meaning 'man of strength'. This ancient name belonged to ten Celtic saints and several legendary heroes. Fergus MacErca led the Gaels from Ireland to Scotland in the fifth century.

Seventeenth-century names

Between 1654 and 1685, 6,500 servants left Bristol to sail to the New World to work for the wealthy owners of cotton plantations in Virginia and the sugar estates of the West Indies. Their names, listed here in order of popularity and in the number of times they appear, provide a rare glimpse into the favourite names of the century.

John (949)
William (648)
Thomas (607)
Richard (457)
Robert (253)
Edward (215)
James (189)
George (177)
Henry (177)
Francis (86)
Samuel (84)
Joseph (82)

Elizabeth (264)
Mary (254)
Anne (217)
Margaret (99)
Joan (98)
Sarah (92)
Jane (82)
Elinor (61)
Alice (50)
Katherine (49)
Susan (37)
Dorothy (31)

Fernanda (G)
Spanish feminine form of Ferdinand, with associations of journey and risk.

Fiammetta (G)
Italian, meaning 'little flame' and often given to redheads.

Fidel (B)
From Latin, meaning 'faithful'.

Fidelia (G)
From Latin, meaning 'faithful'.

Fifi (G)
French pet form of Josephine.

Fingal (B)
From Scottish Gaelic 'fionn gall' or 'fair stranger', which was often used to describe the fair-haired Norwegians. In Irish legend Finn or Fingal was a semi-mythological hero.

Finn (B)
English form of Irish 'fionn', meaning 'fair'. The legendary Irish hero Finn MacCool is said to have erected Giant's Causeway.

Finola (G)
English form of the Irish Gaelic Fionnguala, meaning 'white shoulders'.

Fiona (G)
From Gaelic 'fionn', meaning 'fair', and a name invented by the Scottish writer William Sharp who wrote tales and romances based on Scotland and Ireland's great heroic past. It has become a classic of the 20th century.

Fionnguala (G)
Irish, with the meaning of 'fair shoulders'. In Irish legend the beautiful Fionnguala was the daughter of King Lir.

Fitzroy (B)
Irish, meaning 'son of the king'.

Flann (B)
Irish, meaning 'blood red'. Flann O'Brien is the pen-name of the Irish wit and journalist Brian O'Nolan.

Flavia (G)
From Latin, meaning 'tawny-haired'. Princess Flavia was the heroine of Anthony Hope's swashbuckling tale, *The Prisoner of Zenda* (1898).

Flavian (B)
From Latin, meaning 'tawny-haired'.

Fletcher (B)
From Old French, meaning 'maker of arrows'.

Fleur (G)
French, meaning 'flower'. The name was popular in the 20s and 30s.

Flora (G)

Flora was the goddess of flowers and springtime in ancient Rome. Her name was popular in France at the time of the Renaissance and from here it travelled to Scotland where it became a Christian name for the girls of Clan Macdonald. The most famous Flora of all must surely be Flora Macdonald who helped Bonnie Prince Charlie escape 'over the seas to Skye', although it is thought that Flora referred to herself as 'Florie'.

Flore (G)

Old French, meaning 'flower'. It pre-dates Fleur which is modern French for flower.

Florence (G)

On 4 July 1820 a baby was born of English parents in Italy and was called after the city in which she was born – Florence. (Her sister was less fortunate, being christened Parthenope, the Greek name for her birthplace, Naples.) Florence Nightingale became a national heroine and scores of babies were named after her. The charm of her name has well survived the Victorian era.

Florie (G)

Affectionate form of Flora and Florence. Flora Macdonald was thought to call herself Florie.

Floyd (B)

Popular in the United States and the Caribbean, this is thought to have been an English surname which developed from the Welsh Lloyd – the English having trouble with the Ll – and which was then used as a Christian name in the Americas.

Foster (B)

English surname, like Fletcher, Carter and Smith originating in a trade or profession – in this case, forester. In the 20th century the use of surnames as Christian names has become frequent.

Franca (G)

Italian form of Frances, meaning 'French woman'.

Irish names

It is to the literary and cultural revival of Irish Gaelic at the end of the 19th century, closely linked to nationalism, that the revival of the great Irish names is due. The Act of Union of 1801 imposed by Britain on Ireland was the nail in the coffin of Irish independence, after centuries of occupation by first the Anglo-Normans and subsequently the English. By the mid-19th century the most common Christian names were English: Mary, Margaret and Anne for girls, and John, William and Thomas for boys. The Celtic Renaissance, which began in the last years of the 19th century, encouraged parents to return to the Gaelic names, but it was not until Independence in 1921 that the return of language and names was possible. In the last twenty years Irish names have become immensely popular on both sides of the Irish Sea. While birth columns in the *Irish Times* still include Thomases, Johns and Andrews, they have a strong showing of Conors and Patricks, while girls' names such as Aeife, Aisling, Niamh and Sinéad have been found in the top ten lists for many years.

Girls

Ailbhe (pronounced Al-va)	Elva
Aine (pronounced Orn-ya)	Anne
Aisling (pronounced Ash-leen) means 'dream'	Ashling
Anna (pronounced Orn-na)	Anne
Aoifa (pronounced Eee-fah)	Eva
Bláthnaid (pronounced Blah-naid)	Florence
Bríd (pronounced Breed)	Bridget
Bríde (pronounced Breed-a)	Breda
Ciar (pronounced Keer-a)	Ciara
Dearbháil (pronounced Der-val)	Dervla
Eibhlín (pronounced Eye-leen)	Eileen
Eilia (pronounced Eye-leesh)	Elizabeth
Eimhear (pronounced Eee-ma)	Emer

Eithne (pronounced Eth-nay)	Annie
Fionnuala (pronounced Fin-oo-la)	Finola or Fenella
Gráinne (pronounced Grawn-ya)	Grania
Isabéal (pronounced Isa-bayle)	Isabel
Máire (pronounced Maura, or Moy-ra)	Mary
Mairéad (pronounced Mar-raid)	Margaret
Niamh (pronounced Neeve)	
Orlagh (pronounced Or-la)	Orla
Pádraigín (pronounced Poor-rick-een)	Patricia
Proinséas (pronounced Pron-chas)	Frances
Ríonach (pronounced Ree-on-a)	Riona or Regina
Roisin (pronounced Raw-sheen)	Rosaleen
Síle (pronounced Shee-lar)	Sheila
Sinéad (pronounced Shin-aid)	Jane
Siobhán (pronounced Shev-awn)	Joan
Sorcha (pronounced Sirica)	Sarah

Boys

Ailbhe (pronounced Al-bee)	Alby
Aonghús (pronounced En-guss)	Angus
Bearach (pronounced Ba-ray)	Barry
Breandán (pronounced Bran-dawn)	Brendon
Caoimhín (pronounced Kee-veen)	Kevin
Cathal (pronounced Caah-l)	Charles
Ciarán (pronounced Keer-ran)	Kieran
Conchobhar (pronounced Con-shoy-a)	Conor or Connor
Dáithí (pronounced Daw-hee)	David
Déaglán (pronounced Da-glawn)	Declan
Donal (pronounced Dough-nal)	Donald
Donnchadh (pronounced Don-cah)	Denis
Dubh (pronounced Duv)	Duff
Eamon (pronounced A-mon)	Edmund
Eanna (pronounced Eye-na)	
Fearghal (pronounced Fur-gal)	Fergal
Fearghus (pronounced Fur-gus)	Fergus
Feilim (pronounced Fay-lem)	Felix
Fionn (pronounced Fee-on)	Finn

Fionnbhárr (pronounced Fin-bar)	Finbar
Gairiad (pronounced Gar-a-wed)	Gareth
Gearalt (pronounced Gar-ralt)	Gerald
Giolla Iosa (pronounced Gill-ee-sa)	Giles
Labhrás (pronounced Lao-ras)	Laurence
Liam (pronounced Lee-am)	William
Máirtín (pronounced Mar-teen)	Martin
Micheál (pronounced Mee-haw)	Michael
Néill (pronounced Neel)	Neil
Niall (pronounced Nye-al)	Nial
Pádraic (pronounced Paw-rick)	Patrick
Pádraig (pronounced Paw-drigh)	Patrick
Proinsias (pronounced Pron-schas)	Francis
Risteárd (pronounced Reesh-tard)	Richard
Ruairí (pronounced Roar-ry)	Rory
Séamus (pronounced Shay-mus)	James
Sean (pronounced Shawn)	Shaun
Stiofán (pronounced Stiff-awn)	Stephen
Tadgh (pronounced Tie-ge)	Timothy
Tomas (pronounced To-maas)	Thomas

Frances (B)

English form of medieval Italian Francesca, meaning 'free woman' or 'French woman'. It was first used as a Christian name by the aristocracy in Elizabethan England. In the 18th century the celebrated novelist Frances or Fanny Burney revived its fortunes and it went on to became a favourite Victorian name. It has also become a classic of the 20th century.

Francesca (B)

Italian version of our English Frances. Francesca pre-dates Frances, originating in the 13th century. It came into use in England in the late 50s.

Francesco (B)

Italian forerunner of Francis. Francesco was the nickname given to St Francis of Assisi by his father because of the number of journeys he made to France. It means 'little Frenchman'.

Francine (G)
French diminutive of Françoise, meaning 'little French woman'.

Francis (B)
From Italian and French, meaning 'free man' or 'French man'. The name was in use as a Christian name by the 16th century, its most famous bearers being Francis Drake and Francis Bacon, both of whom were members of the aristocratic Russell family. In this century the spelling Frances is preferred.

Françoise (G)
French form of Frances, meaning 'French woman'.

Frank (B)
Frank pre-dates Francis as a name, although in the 19th century it was used as a shortened form of Francis. It came directly from the Old German name for the French, the Franks, or 'free men'.

Franklin (B)
A surname that became a Christian name in the United States in memory of Benjamin Franklin.

Fraser (B)
Scottish surname which has been used as a Christian name since the 50s.

Freda (G)
German and Austrian feminine form of Frederick, although it is also used as a short form of the Old English name Winifred.

Frédéric (B)
French version of Frederick.

Frederick (B)
Anglo-Saxon and Old German, with the associations of 'peace' and 'rule', it is one of England's oldest names. Freddy Eynsford Hill, who falls in love with Eliza Doolittle, in George Bernard Shaw's *Pygmalion* (1913) confirmed it

as an Edwardian favourite.

Frederika (G)
Pretty Dutch and German feminine form of Frederick which has a mildly aristocratic feel.

Freya (G)
Scandinavian, meaning 'lady'.

Fyodor (B)
Russian version of the Greek Theodore, meaning 'God's gift'.

G

Gabriel (B)
From Hebrew, meaning 'strong man of God'. Its biblical associations caused it to be used a great deal in the Middle Ages, sometimes as Gabel, but less so since. A significant 19th-century Gabriel was Gabriel Oak in Thomas Hardy's *Far from the Madding Crowd*, so-called because of his reliable character.

Gabriella (G)
Italian feminine form of Gabriel which has been used in England in the last 40 years. The French form is Gabrielle, and the pet form of both is Gigi.

Gaia (G)
Greek, meaning 'earth' and the name of the ancient earth goddess.

Gail (G)
Short form of Abigail, meaning 'a father's joy' which has become a name in its own right in the 20th century.

Gareth (B)
From Welsh 'gwaredd', meaning 'gentle'. It was popularized by Tennyson's poem of the Arthurian romance 'Gareth and Lynette' (1872).

Garfield (B)
From Anglo-Saxon, with associations of spear and field, originally a surname.

Gary (B)
Short form of both Gareth and Garfield which has almost become a name in its own right. The popularity of the name is attributed to Hollywood actor Gary Cooper who was actually named Frank.

Gaston (B)
Old French, meaning 'guest'. A name favoured in France by aristocrats and commoners alike.

Gavin (B)
Scottish form of French Norman Gauvain or Gawain, with the meaning of 'hawker of the plains', dating at least from the end of the 17th century.

Gawen (B)
Modern Welsh form of 'Gwalchmai' or 'Gawain', meaning 'hawker of the plains'. In Welsh legend Gawain was a nephew of King Arthur and a Knight of the Round Table. Tennyson revived the story of Gawain and the Green Knight.

Gay (G)
Short form of Gaynor, itself an English rendering of the Welsh 'Gwenhwyuns' or 'Guinevere', meaning 'fair'. An alternative spelling is Gaye.

Gayle (G)
American modern spelling of Gail, both originally derived from Abigail, meaning 'a father's joy'.

Geena (G)
Hindu, meaning 'silvery'.

Gemma (G)
Italian, with the meaning of 'precious stone'. It appears in 13th-century records in England, but was not revived until this century. It was the 20th most popular name for girls in Scotland in 1990.

Genevieve (G)
Modern French from Old French Genovefa. Coleridge wrote a sonnet 'Genevieve' which brought the name to public attention. It is still widely used.

Genovefa (G)
Old French, with the associations of people and woman. St Genovefa, who lived in the fifth century, is the patron saint of Paris.

Geoffrey (B)
From Old German, meaning 'peace of God'. Common in

the Middle Ages, with two well-known namesakes, Geoffrey of Monmouth and Geoffrey Chaucer, the name came back into fashion in the 19th century.

Geordie (B)
Scottish and Northumberland form of George, also used now as a nickname for a Tynesider.

George (B)
From Greek, meaning 'tiller of the ground' or 'farmer'. St George in legend slayed a dragon to save a princess and was adopted as a patron saint of England by the Crusaders who brought his name back from the East in the 14th century. It did not come into proper usage until the 19th century. A popular Edwardian Christian name, it is happily now undergoing a revival of fortunes.

Georgette (G)
French feminine form of George.

Georgia (G)
Like Virginia and Carolina, Georgia has always been popular in the United States, and in recent years has leapt in popularity in England. Its origins, happily, may be English: a godchild of Anne of Denmark, the wife of James I, was christened Georgia Anna.

Georgiana (G)
18th-century feminine form of George popularized by 'sweet-natured Georgiana Spencer', celebrated beauty and wife of the fifth Duke of Devonshire (born 1757).

Georgina (G)
18th-century feminine form of George which has become popular in the present century.

Geraint (B)
Welsh form of Latin Gerontius, meaning 'old'.

Gerald (B)
From Old German, with the associations of 'spear' and 'force'. The name passed into Italian, and the Fitzgerald family, who originally came from Florence, were called Gerhadrini. As the earls of Kildare they were the most powerful landowners in Ireland for many centuries. The

name also exists in Wales at Gerallt, but it was from Ireland that it passed into English usage in the 19th century.

Geraldine (G)
Feminine form of Gerald invented by the 16th-century poet Surrey to celebrate the beauty of Lady Elizabeth Fitzgerald, whom he addressed as 'Geraldine'. In the 19th century it was a popular Christian name in both Ireland and England.

Gerard (B)
Old German, with associations of 'hard spear', suggesting it was a name given to battle heroes. It was a popular Norman name, and passed into modern French, and is listed in the Domesday Book, although in later centuries it was replaced by Gerald.

Gerda (G)
Old Norse, meaning 'shielded'. In Norse mythology, Gerda was the wife of the ancient deity, Ing. It became popular in England after the publication of Hans Christian Andersen's *The Snow Queen*.

Germaine (B&G)
Latin, meaning 'from Germany' and originally a boy's name. There were two early French saints one of whom gave his name to the area of St Germain in Paris.

Gerry (B)
Familiar form of Gerald and Gerard.

Gertrude (G)
Name from Old Norse mythology. Gertrude was one of the Valkyries who took the bodies of dead heroes to heaven. Shakespeare gave the name to Hamlet's mother. In this century the actress Gertrude Lawrence, who was born of Anglo-Danish parents, popularized the name.

Gervase (B)
Old German name, with associations of spear and servant, introduced to England by the Normans.

Ghislaine (G)
Old French form of Giselle, meaning 'pledge'. It is pronounced Ger-lain.

Giacomo (B)
Italian form of James and Jacob, from the Latin 'Jacomus'.

Gigi (G)
Pet form of Gabriella and Gabrielle.

Gilbert (B)
Old German, meaning 'bright pledge' and the name of both a Scottish and English saint. It was a common name in the Middle Ages, and revived at the end of the 19th century for its religious and historical associations.

Gilberta (G)
Feminine form of Gilbert.

Gilbertine (G)
French feminine form of Gilbert.

Giles (B)
Of two origins, both extremely old. There was a Celtic name Gille, meaning 'servant' but Giles also has Greek and Latin origins. St Giles was a favourite English saint in the Middle Ages. The name fell out of use in the 16th century but has become popular again in recent decades.

Gill (G)
Shortened form of Gillian, dating from the Middle Ages.

Gillian (G)
Medieval form of Juliana, a classic of the times.

Gilroy (B)
Gaelic, meaning 'servant of the red-haired man'.

Gina (G)
Used in English as a shortened form of Georgina. The actress Gina Lollobrigida popularized the name in the 50s.

Ginny (G)
Short form of Virginia.

Giselle (G)
Old German and French, meaning 'pledge'.

Gladys (G)
Welsh royal name meaning 'ruler'. It came into use in English in the 1890s after appearing in a novel of the time.

Glen (B)
Celtic/Gaelic name, meaning 'valley'.

Glenda (G)
English form of the Welsh Gwenda, meaning 'holy good'. Its Welsh associations made it popular in Australia.

Glenn (G)
Modern girl's name from Glen, meaning 'valley' which first appeared in the United States.

Glenys (G)
Welsh, meaning 'valley'. An alternative spelling is Glenis.

Gloria (G)
Latin, meaning 'glory'. George Bernard Shaw is responsible for its popularity in this century. He gave it to a character in his play *You Never Can Tell* (1898).

Glyn (B)
Favourite Welsh boys' name, meaning 'valley'.

Glynis (G)
Welsh name, meaning 'valley', popular in the 20s.

Godfrey (B)
Old German, meaning 'God-peace'. It was revived in the 19th century as a heroic medieval name.

Gordon (B)
A clan surname, deriving from a place in Berwickshire, which became a Christian name through its association with General Gordon of Khartoum in 1885. It was continually in the Scottish top 30 until the 80s.

Grace (G)
From Latin 'gratia' meaning 'grace' and a favourite with the Puritans who were very fond of names which described virtuous characteristics. For this reason it passed out of use in the more rumbustious 18th century, but returned in the Victorian era following the heroic deeds of Grace Darling.

Graeme (B)
From Greum, the Gaelic form of Graham and the name of a powerful family of the Scottish Lowlands. It is now the most popular spelling of the name in Scotland.

Graham (B)

English spelling of Greum, or Graeme, and the name of a powerful family of the Scottish Lowlands who took their name from the Lincolnshire town of Grantham, whence they originated, after they were granted lands in the north by William the Conqueror. Used as a Christian name in the 19th century and was popular in the 40s and 50s.

Gráinne (G)

Irish, meaning 'love'. Gráinne, Queen of Tara, eloped with the legendary Diarmaid in Irish legend.

Grania (G)

English rendering of Irish Gráinne, meaning 'love'. It is now quite common outside Ireland.

Grant (B)

From French 'le grand', literally 'the tall man'. A surname which became a popular American Christian name through its association with Ulysses S Grant, 18th President of the United States and used in England since the mid-50s.

Gregory (B)

From Greek 'gregorios', meaning 'the watchman', one the great names of the early Byzantine Church and subsequently the name of 16 popes. Out of use in England for many centuries, it was revived at the end of the 19th century and has been in more or less continual use since.

Greta (G)

Swedish form of Margaret, sometimes spelt Gretta. It was popularized by the 'divine' Garbo.

Gretchen (G)

German pet form of Margaret. Gretel, which is similar, has the same root.

Griffith (B)

From Old Welsh Gruffudd, meaning 'lord', a name associated with royalty and often found in the Welsh Marches. The short form is Griff.

Griselda (G)

From Old German, with associations of battle. Introduced in the Middle Ages, it became very popular in Scotland.

Spring feast days

March
1 St David of Wales, St Felix 2 St Chad 4 St Adrian
and his Companions, St Casimir, St Peter
5 St Adrian, St John Joseph, St Kieran of Saighir
6 St Colette, St Cyril of Constantinople, St Felicity
8 St Felix of Dunwich, St John, St Julian, St Stephen
9 St Catharine of Bologna, St Frances, St Gregory
10 St Anastasia Patricia 11 St Benedict, St
Constantine of Cornwall, St Oengus or Aengus the
Culdee 12 St Bernard, St Maximilian, St Seraphina
13 St Gerald 14 St Matilda 15 St Louise, St Lucretia,
St Zachary 16 St Finian Lobhair, St Julian
17 St Gertrude, St Joseph of Arimathea, St Patrick of
Ireland, St Paul 18 St Alexander and St Cyril of
Jerusalem, St Edward the Martyr 19 St Joseph
(husband of the Virgin) 20 St Cuthbert, St Herbert,
St Martin 22 St Basil, St Nicholas Owen, St Paul
23 St Benedict 24 St Catharine, St William of
Norwich 25 St Lucy, St Margaret Clitherow
26 St Basil the Younger, St Felix 27 St John of
Egypt 29 St Gwladys, St Rupert 30 St Leonard
31 St Balbina, St Benjamin and St Guy.

April
1 St Catharine of Palma, St Gilbert of Caithness,
St Hugh 2 St Francis, St Mary of Egypt 3 St Irene, St
Richard 4 St Benedict, St Isidore of Seville
5 St Albert, St Geraldv 7 St George the Younger,
St Henry Walpole, St Herman Joseph 8 St Julia
Billiart, St Walter 9 St Hugh 10 St Michael
11 St Gemma, St Isaac 12 St Julius 13 St Martin
14 St Bernard, St John, St Lambert 15 St Anastasia,
St Basilissa 16 St Bernadette, St Magnus of Orkney
19 St Leo, St Agnes, St Hildegund, St Marian
21 St Anselm of Canterbury, St Conrada
22 St Theodore, St Leonides 23 St George, St Gerard
24 St Ives or Ivo, St William 25 St Mark the

Evangelist 26 St Franca, St Peter, St Stephen
27 St Castor, St Stephen. 28 St Cyril, St Louis,
St Theodora, St Valeria 29 St Catherine of Sienna,
St Hugh, St Wilfrid the Younger.

May
1 St Peregrine, St Sigismund 3 St Philip the Apostle,
St James the Less, St Timothy 5 St Hilary 6 St Edbert
7 St John of Beverley 8 St Benedict, St Victor
10 St Solange, St John and Avila 11 St Francis,
St Walter 12 St Dominic 13 St Andrew, St John,
St Solomon 14 St Mary Mazzarello 15 St Bertha,
St Rupert, St Hilary 16 St Brendan, St Simon Stock
17 St Bruno, St Pascal 18 St Elgiva, St Eric
(King of Sweden), St Felix, St John 1 19 St Crispin,
St Dunstan 20 St Basilla 21 St Andrew Bobola
22 St Helen of Caernarvon, St Julia, St Rita
(Margharita) 23 St William of Rochester.
24 St David 1 of Scotland, St Vincent 25 St Leo,
St Madeleine Sophie 26 St Lambert, St Mariana,
St Philip Neri St Julius 28 St William 29 St Bernard,
St Cyril, St Theodosia of Constantinople 30 St
Ferdinand of Castile, St Joan of Arc, St Walstan
31 St Petronilla.

Guy (B)
From Old German 'wido', meaning 'wide' which passed
into Italian as Guido and French Norman as Guy. It arrived
in England at the time of the Conqueror and was a popular
name until it was more or less prohibited from use after
Guy Fawkes. Sir Walter Scott revived its fortunes when he
published *Guy Mannering* in 1815.

Gwen (G)
Short form of Gwendolen, meaning 'fair' and 'beautiful'.

Gwenan (G)

Welsh, an affectionate form of Gwendolen, meaning 'fair' and 'beautiful'.

Gwenda (G)

From Old Welsh 'guenddoleu', meaning 'fair and good'.

Gwendolen (G)

English form of the Old Welsh 'guenddoleu', meaning 'white circle', perhaps in reference to an ancient moon goddess. The name appears in Welsh legends many times. It passed into English as Gwendolen, or Gwendolyn, at the end of the 19th century and has been in use ever since.

Gwenonwy (G)

Welsh, meaning 'lily of the valley'.

Gwyn (B)

Welsh, meaning 'fair'.

Gwyneth (G)

From Old Welsh 'gwynnedd', meaning 'blessed' or 'happy'.

H

Hadwen (G)
Welsh, meaning 'summer beautiful'.

Haidee (G)
Modern Greek, meaning 'caressed'. Byron first used the name in his epic poem 'Don Juan'.

Hal (B)
Medieval affectionate form of Henry.

Haldane (B)
Old Anglo-Scandinavian name, meaning 'half-dane' – found in north of England.

Haman (B)
Hebrew, meaning 'gracious'.

Hamilton (B)
Scottish place and clan name, occasionally used as a Christian name north of the border.

Hamish (B)
Scottish rendering of the Irish Séamus, which itself corresponds to James, with the meaning of 'one who supplants'. Hamish had a long pedigree in the Highlands but came into general use in the 19th century when there was a vogue for Scottish names.

Hank (B)
American shortened form of Henry derived from the Dutch Henk or Hendrick.

Hannah (G)
Hebrew, meaning 'favoured by God'. In the Old Testament, Hannah was the mother of the prophet Samuel. The Puritans loved biblical names and Hannah became a great favourite of the 17th century and has been in more or less continual use since, even undergoing a surge

Summary feast days

June

1 St Candida, St Inigo, St Justin, St Winstan;
2 St Stephen 3 St Clothilde, St Isaac, St Kevin or
Coemgen 4 St Francis 5 St Boniface 6 St Claud,
St Philip 7 St Anthony, St Paul 8 St Cloud of Metz,
St William of York 9 St Columba of Iona, St Vincent
11 St Barnabas 12 St Antonina, St Leo, St Odulf,
St Paula 13 St Antony of Padua 14 St Dogmael
15 St Alice, St Germaine 16 St Cyr 17 St Emily,
St Herve, St Teresa, St Sanchia 18 St Elisabeth,
St Gregory 19 St Boniface, St Gervase, St Juliana,
St Odo, St Romauld 20 St John 21 St Alban 22
St Thomas More 23 St Ethelreda or Audrey,
St Agrippina, St Thomas Garnet 24 St Bartholomew,
St John the Baptist, St Ralph 25 St Thea, St William
26 St John of the Goths 27 St Cyril, St George
Mtasmindeli, St Samson 28 St Sergius 29 St Cassius,
St Paul the Apostle, St Peter the Apostle, St Salome,
St Judith 30 St Bertrand, St Emma.

July

1 St Aaron, St Oliver Plunket 2 St Otto 3 St Leo,
St Thomas the Apostle 4 St Andrew of Crete,
St Bertha, St Odo 6 St Dominica, St Modwenna
7 St Cyril, St Hedda of Winchester 8 St Adrian,
St Priscilla, St Kilian, St Raymund of Toulouse
9 St Veronica 10 St Felicity 11 St Benedict, St Olga
12 St Felix, St Jason 13 St Bridget and Maura,
St Mildred, St Silas 14 Bastille Day 15 St David,
St Donald, St Edith, St Swithin 16 St Helier 17
St Clement, St Kenelm, St Leo, St Marcellina
18 St Bruno, St Frederick 19 St Ambrose,
St James 20 St Gregory, St Margaret 21 St Laurence,
St Victor 22 St Mary Magdalen, St Philip Evans
23 St Anne or Susanna, St Bridget of Sweden
24 St Boris, St Christina, St Declan, St Lewinna

25 St Christopher, St Valentina 26 St Anne
27 St Aurelia, St Natalia 29 St Beatrice, St Martha,
St Olav 30 St Julitta 31 St Helen, St Justin, St Neot.

August

1 St Aled, St Alphonse 2 St Stephen 3 St Thomas of
Dover 5 St Afra, St Nonna 6 St Justus 7 St Claudia,
St Albert 8 St Dominic 9 St Oswald of Northumbria
10 St Laurence of Rome 11 St Alexander, St Clare
of Assisi, St Leila, St Susanna 13 St Cassian,
St Radegund, Queen of Thuringia 14 St Maximilian
15 Assumption of the Virgin Mary 16 St Stephen of
Hungary 17 St Clare, St Hyacinth 18 St Beatrice,
St Helena 19 St Andrew, St Louis of Anjou,
St Thecla 20 St Oswin, St Ronald 21 St Abraham
22 St Sigfrid 23 St Eugene, St Rose of Lima,
St Tydfil 24 St Bartholomew 25 St Gregory,
St Joan, St Patricia, St Louis 26 St Elizabeth, St John,
St Teresa 27 Little St Hugh, St Monica
28 St Alexander, St Augustine, St Edmund,
St Julian 29 St Edwold, St Sabina 30 St Felix,
St Margaret 31 St Aidan of Lindisfarne.

in popularity in the last decade. The Greek form of Hannah
is Anna.

Hannibal (B)
Phoenician, meaning 'grace of Baal' and the name of the
great Carthaginian general who led elephants over the Alps.
Surprisingly it was a popular name in Cornwall for a
number of centuries.

Hanno (B)
Phoenician, meaning 'grace'.

Hans (B)
German equivalent of John, it comes straight from the
Hebrew Johannes.

Harald (B)
Scandinavian name, meaning 'ruler of the army'. It dates from the tenth century and has longstanding royal associations.

Hardy (B)
Old French, with the association of bravery.

Harold (B)
Recorded in Anglo-Saxon literature as Hereweald, meaning 'army power', it was the name of the last Anglo-Saxon king, Harold II who was defeated in 1066 just before the Norman Conquest. Revived in the 19th century when Saxon names came back into fashion it was also a popular Edwardian Christian name.

Haroun (B)
Arabic form of the Egyptian name Aaron, meaning 'high mountain'.

Harriet (G)
English form of the French Henriette, meaning 'little ruler'. The name Henriette was first brought to England by Charles I's French wife Henrietta Maria. The English court, finding the pronunciation difficult, called her 'Hawyot', from which Harriet eventually emerged. It was popular in the 18th and early 19th century and has been in more or less steady use in the present century.

Harry (B)
Earliest English form of Henry, meaning 'ruler'. In the present century it has almost become a name in its own right. This befits its history, since it was from the French Henri (pronounced En-ri) that it was first created in the Middle Ages.

Harvey (B)
From the French Hervé, meaning 'army warrior'. The name came to England with the Normans but within a few centuries it had died out in England, except in Yorkshire.

Hassan (B)
Arabic, meaning 'handsome'.

Hayden (B&G)
Old Celtic and Welsh, meaning 'fire'. Originally a boy's name, it has also been used as a girl's name in recent times. An alternative spelling is Haydn.

Hayley (G)
English surname which first came into use as a Christian name in the Mills family. Hayley Mills was born in 1944 and named after her mother Mary Hayley Bell.

Hazel (G)
Coined in the 19th century when there was a fashion for botanical names, although there were much older associations since the hazel was the ancient Celtic fruit of wisdom. The French for hazel was 'aveline' which became Evelyn in English.

Heather (G)
English botanical name which came into use, along with its Latin name Erica, in the 19th century when there was a fashion for plant and flower names. Heather has been in the top 40 names for girls in Scotland since 1958.

Hebe (G)
Greek, meaning 'youthfulness' and pronounced He-bee. In Greek mythology, Hebe was the goddess of eternal life and handed the cup bearing the elixir of youthfulness to the gods.

Hector (B)
From Greek, meaning 'steadfast'. In Greek legend he was the valiant son of King Priam of Troy. His name passed into French in the Middle Ages and subsequently to the Scottish court. A longstanding Highland name, it came to England towards the end of the last century when there was a revival of interest in classical names.

Hedda (G)
From Old German, meaning 'strife'.

Heddwen (G)
Welsh, meaning 'blessed peace'.

Heddwyn (B)
Welsh, meaning 'blessed peace'.

Hedy (G)
Pet form of a very old German name, Hedwig, meaning 'refuge in war'. It was popularized in the 30s by Hedy Lamarr.

Heidi (G)
Austrian short form of Adelheid, popularized by Johanna Spyri's children's classics.

Helen (G)
From Greek, meaning 'the bright one'. In Greek legend, Helen was the wife of Menelaus, famous for her exquisite beauty, who eloped with Paris to Troy. It was also a saintly name of the early Byzantine Church, and St Helena was the mother of Emperor Constantine. Despite these associations, it did not come into use until the Renaissance and its real popularity has been a largely 20th-century phenomenon, the result of a revival of classical Greek and Roman names at the end of the 19th century. The French form is Hélène.

Helena (G)
Latin form of the Greek Helen, meaning 'the bright one'. St Helena was the mother of Constantine the Great, the first Christian Emperor of Byzantium. In religious legend St Helena is said to have discovered the site of Calvary. The Renaissance brought the name into use across Europe for its classical associations and Shakespeare has two Helenas, the Athenian lady in love with Demetrius in *A Midsummer Night's Dream*, and a girl protected by the mother of Bertram in *All's Well That Ends Well*. It is a name held in particular affection in Scotland.

Helga (G)
Old Norse, meaning 'holy'. Olga is the Russian form of the name.

Helmut (B)
From Old German, meaning 'famous for courage'.

Heloïse (G)
Medieval French form of the Old German Helewidis, meaning 'healthy'. The love story of Heloïse and Abelard is a classic of French courtly romances.

Henrietta (G)

French feminine form of Henry, meaning 'little ruler'. The name was introduced to England by Henriette Marie, French wife of Charles I and had been coined for her by her father Henri IV of France. It was quickly adopted by the aristocracy, Oliver Cromwell even choosing it as a name for one of his daughters – but pronounced Haw-y-ot by the English tongue and out of this the more popular Harriet grew. Henrietta, however, was revived in the 19th century and has remained in use, even experiencing something of a revival in the last 30 years. The American form is Henriet.

Henry (B)

From French Henri, which derived from the Old German Hainrich, meaning 'ruler', suggesting that it was always a royal name. It passed into English as Herry or Harry in the Middle Ages, with the written Latin form Henricus. There were eight English kings called Henry between the 11th and 16th centuries. The name was revived at the end of the 18th century and has remained popular.

Hepzibar (G)

Hebrew, meaning 'my delight is in her'. In the Old Testament Hepzibar is the wife of Hezekiah. Although popular among Jews for many centuries it only came into use in England with the Puritans. The short form is Hepsie.

Herbert (B)

Norman courtly surname which passed to the English Herbert family in the Middle Ages. It came into use as a Christian name in the 19th century for its aristocratic associations.

Hereward (B)

Anglo-Saxon, with the associations of army and protection, indicating that it was a royal name. Hereward the Wake, the last Saxon leader, fought against the Normans in the 11th century. The name came into use in the 19th century when there was a fashion for Saxon heroic names, although it has not passed into the present century.

Herman (B)

From Old German, meaning 'army man'. The French form is Armand.

Autumn feast days

September

1 St Verena, St Giles 2 St Antonius, St Castor
3 St Gregory, St Phoebe 4 St Ida, St Rosalie,
St Rose 5 St Laurence, St Theodore 7 St Cloud,
St John 8 St Adrian, St Natalia, St Nestor
9 St Ciaran or Kieran 10 St Aubert, St Finnian
11 St Peter, St Theodora 12 St Guy 15 St Catherine
of Genoa 16 St Cornelius, St Cyprian, St Edith,
St Ludmilla 17 St Columba, St Francis, St Hildegard,
St Robert 18 St Joseph 19 St Emily, St Mary,
St Susanna, St Theodore 20 St Candida, St Philippa
21 St Matthew, St Maura' St Michael 22 St Felix,
St Maurice 23 St Adamnan or Eunan of Iona,
St Andrew 24 St Gerard, St Robert Flower of Knares-
borough 25 St Albert, St Finbar, St Vincent
26 St Damian, St Teresa, 27 St Barrog or Barnoch,
St Vincent 28 St Wencelaus of Bohema 29 St Gabriel,
St Michael and St Raphael (archangels)
30 St Gregory, St Jerome, St Simon.

October

1 St Thérèse of Lisieux 2 St Leger 3 St Gerard,
St Ewald, St Thomas Cantelupe 4 St Francis of Assisi
5 St Flora 6 St Bruno, St Faith 7 St Justina, St Mark
8 St Demetrius 9 St Denis of Paris, St Ghislain, St
Louis 10 St Daniel, St Paulinus of York 11 St Alex-
ander, St Canice or Kenneth 12 St Edwin, St Felix, St
Wilfrid of York 13 St Edward the Confessor, St Gerald
14 St Dominic 15 St Leonard, St Teresa of Avila,
St Thecla 16 St Bertrand, St Gerard 18 St Gwen of
Cornwall, St Luke 19 St Cleopatra, St Phillip Howard
20 St Andrew of Crete, St Bertilla 22 St Philip 23 St
John 24 St Antony, St Felix, St Martin 25 St Crispin
26 St Cedd 27 St Odhran of Iona 28 St Abraham,
St Anastasia, St Cyril, St Jude 31 St Bee, St Quentin.

November

1 All Saints' Day 3 St Hubert, St Malachy,
St Winifred or Gwenfrewi 4 St Charles, St John
5 St Bertilla, St Elisabeth 6 St Melanie, St Leonard
9 St Theodore 10 St Leo the Great
11 St Bartholomew, St Martin 12 St Astrik,
St Cumian 13 St Brice, St Frances 14 St Laurence,
St Nicholas, St Stephen 15 St Albert, St Leopold,
St Malo 16 St Agnes, St Edmund St Margaret of
Scotland 17 St Victoria, St Elizabeth, St Gregory,
St Hugh of Lincoln 18 St Odo 20 St Edmund,
St Felix 21 St Albert 22 St Cecilia 24 St Flora,
St Mary 25 St Moses 26 St Basle, St Silvester,
St Conrad 27 St Fergus, St James 28 St Catherine,
St James, St Stephen 29 St Brendan 30 St Andrew the
Apostle, St Cuthbert.

Hermia (G)

From Greek, with the association of messenger. Shakespeare coined the name for one of his Athenian ladies in *A Midsummer Night's Dream*.

Hermione (G)

From Greek, meaning 'of the god Hermes'. In Greek legend, Hermione was the daughter of Helen of Troy and Menelaus. Shakespeare chose the name for the queen in *The Winter's Tale* and it was revived at the end of the 19th century for its classical and Shakespearean associations.

Hester (G)

English form of the Persian Esther coined by the Puritans in the 17th century for its biblical associations. It was also an aristocratic name, its most famous bearer Lady Hester Stanhope, niece of William Pitt who travelled in the Levant and lived with the Bedouin of Palmyra.

Hilary (B & G)
From Greek, meaning 'cheerful'. In medieval times it was used as a boy's and girl's name and was revived in the 19th century for its classical associations. It was a particuarly popular name for girls in the 50s.

Hilda (G)
Old English, meaning 'battle maiden' and a name which has long been associated with the north of England. St Hilda was the seventh-century founder and abbess of Whitby Abbey and the name has stayed in use in the area for over 1,000 years. It was revived in the 19th century for its historical and religious feel and was a popular name in the first half of this century.

Hildegarde (G)
An Old German name, meaning 'one who knows battle'.

Hiram (B)
Hebrew, meaning 'exalted brother', Hiram was a common name in England in the 17th century and is still sometimes used in Yorkshire. In the Old Testament Hiram was the King of Tyre who supplied cedar wood to David and Solomon.

Holly (G)
Delightful English plant name that became popular at the end of the 19th century.

Homer (B)
From Greek, meaning 'security'.

Honesty (G)
One of the virtue names coined by the Puritans in the 17th century.

Honor (G)
From Latin, meaning 'honour'. Although a favourite virtue name of the Puritans, it had a much longer history, appearing in medieval records as Honora, as well as Onora and Annora. The 18th-century form was Honoria.

Hope (G)
Puritan virtue name dating from the 17th century which has been especially popular in the United States.

Horace (B)

From Latin, meaning 'keeper of the hours' and the name of one of ancient Rome's greatest poets. It first came into use during the Renaissance and was kept in use in literary and aristocratic circles until the present century.

Horatia (G)

Feminine form of Horatio. Nelson, whose first name was Horatio, and Lady Hamilton christened their daughter Horatia.

Horatio (B)

Italian, meaning 'keeper of the hours'.

Howard (B)

Surname that became a popular Christian name in the 19th century. The Howards were dukes of Norfolk and their surname was coined for its aristocratic feel.

Howell (B)

From Welsh 'hywel', meaning 'eminent'.

Hu (B)

Old Celtic form of the modern Hugh, it has the meaning of fire or inspiration. Hu Gadarn, 'the Mighty', was a hero of Celtic legend.

Hubert (B)

A popular name in France and Belgium on account of an eighth-century St Hubert, it appeared briefly in England in the 19th century.

Hugh (B)

One of the ancient Celtic names, meaning 'fire' or 'inspiration'. Although a popular medieval name and the name of an important English saint, the name fell into disuse in later centuries. Happily it was revived in the 19th century and has been in more or less continuous use since, even experiencing something of a boom in the 80s and 90s.

Hugo (B)

Latin form of Hugh, introduced by the Normans which was revived at the end of the 19th century when there was a fashion for classical names.

Humfrey (B)

From the Old German Hunfrid, meaning 'peaceful giant'. It was introduced to England by the Normans as a knightly and noble name but has not survived. Humphrey is a relatively modern spelling.

Huw (B)

Modern Welsh spelling of the ancient Hu, meaning 'fire' or 'inspiration'. Hu Gadarn was a hero of Celtic legend.

Hywel (B)

Welsh royal name, meaning 'eminent', which is also written and pronounced in the English fashion Howel. It is an ancient name, found also in Breton legend as Hoel, King Hoel being an ally and relative of King Arthur.

I

Iain (B)
Highlands version of John, the name came to Scotland as the Dutch Jan (pronounced 'Yan') in the late Middle Ages. The original John O'Groats seems to have been a Jan de Groot who built a house at the tip of Northeast Scotland in the reign of James IV. It became a popular Highland name and was adopted, with this spelling and as Ian, by the English in the 19th century.

Ian (B)
English spelling of the original Highland Iain. Ian became a common name in the 19th century and has become a classic of the 20th.

Ianthe (G)
From Greek, meaning 'a violet'. In Greek legend, Ianthe was a sea nymph, daughter of the god Oceanus.

Ida (G)
From Old Norse, meaning 'hard worker'. Ida appears in the Domesday Book, suggesting that it is a very old name, but was out of use for many centuries. It was revived by Tennyson in his poem 'The Princess' (1847) and was popular among the Victorians.

Idina (G)
Old Norse, meaning 'work'. A prettier version of Ida.

Idris (B)
From Old Welsh, meaning 'fiery Lord'. Idris Gawr or Idris the Giant was a legendary astronomer and magician. The mountain Cader Idris is said to be his observatory.

Iduna (G)
Iduna was the Norse goddess of springtime and guardian of the golden apples which held the promise of eternal youth.

Ievan (B)
An alternative spelling of Evan, the Welsh equivalent of John.

Ifan (B)
Old Welsh name which, like Ievan, is sometimes used as an equivalent of John but is actually a name in its own right, meaning 'young warrior'.

Ifor (B)
Although this is correctly thought of as a Welsh name, it also appears in Old Breton, suggesting that it was a common Celtic kingly name. It means 'lord'.

Ike (B)
American short form of Isaac, from the Hebrew 'Yitschak', meaning 'laughter'.

Ileana (G)
Russian version of Eleanor.

Ilona (G)
Russian version of Helen.

Ilse (G)
Scandinavian and German version of Elizabeth which is popular in Northern Europe. It has the association of 'promise of God' from its Hebrew original. It was immortalized by Ingrid Bergman in *Casablanca*.

Imma (G)
Saxon form of Emma.

Immanuel (B)
Alternative spelling of Emanuel, from the Hebrew, meaning 'God is with us'.

Imogen (G)
Literary name, coined by Shakespeare for a young girl in his play *Cymbeline*. There is a story that he originally called her Innogen, which means 'innocence', but that it was misread by the printers and Imogen was the result.

India (G)
Name coined by the Mountbatten family for Lady India Hicks, granddaughter of Lord Mountbatten, India's last viceroy before Independence in 1947.

Ines (G)
Spanish version of Agnes, meaning 'pure' or 'sacred'.

Inge (G)
A shortened form of Ingrid, which is used as a name in its own right in Scandinavia.

Ingrid (G)
Old Norse name which is still in use in Sweden and which came to England at the time of the Danish invasions as Ingrede. It died out but has been revived in this century, mainly through the popularity of the film star Ingrid Bergman.

Inigo (B)
Welsh form of the Latin Ignatius, best known because of the architect, Inigo Jones.

Iolanthe (G)
Greek, meaning 'a violet'.

Iona (G)
Also written Ione, it refers to the ancient island off Mull. The singer Donovan named his daughter Ione Skye.

Ira (B)
Aramaic, meaning 'stallion'. Ira was a priest of David in the Old Testament.

Irene (G)
From Greek 'eirene', meaning 'peace'. It came into use at the end of the 19th century for its classical associations, being properly pronounced Eye-reen-ee. In the present century the American pronunciation Eye-reen has supplanted the classical.

Iris (G)
From Greek, meaning 'rainbow'. In classical mythology, Iris was the rainbow bridge who permitted messages to be carried from the gods to the mortals. The name came into use at the end of the 19th century when there was a fashion for classical names, but also because it was a flower name, the iris being so called for its rainbow variety of colours.

Winter feast days

December

1 St Alexander, St Edmund Campion, St Ralph
Sherwin 2 St Viviana 3 St Cassian, St Claudius,
St Francis Xavier 4 St Osmund 5 St Crispin
6 St Abraham, St Nicholas 7 St Ambrose, St Martin
10 St Edmund, St Eustace 11 St Daniel 12 St Finnian
13 St Lucy, St Othilia 15 St Paul 16 St Adelaide
19 St Gregory, St Timothy 20 St Dominic 21 St John,
St Peter 22 St Flavian 23 St Victoria 24 St Adela
25 Christmas Day, St Anastasia and St Eugenia
26 St Stephen 27 St Fabiola, St John the Evangelist
28 St Antony, St Theodore 29 St Thomas of
Canterbury 30 St Anysia 31 St Columba, St Melania,
St Silvester.

January

New Year's Day, St Felix, St Peter, St William;
2 St Basil, St Caspar, St Gregory 3 St Genevieve or
Genovefa of Paris, St Peter Balsam; 4 St Elizabeth
Bayley Seton, St Gregory, St Roger 5 St Simeon
Stylites; 6 St John 7 St Lucian, St Raymund
9 St Marciana, St Peter 10 St Dermot or Diarmaid,
St William 12 St Benedict, St Tatiana 13 St Hilary
14 St Antony Pucci, St Felix, St Kentigern or Mungo,
15 St Isidore 16 St Priscilla 18 St Peter's Chair, Rome
19 St Albert, St Charles, St Messalina 20 St Sebastian
21 St Agnes, St Alban or Bartholomew Roe
22 St Dominic, St Vincent; 23 St Clement, St John
25 Burns Night and Conversion of St Paul
26 Australia Day, Republic Day India and St Conan of
Man, St Margarete of Hungary, St Paula, St Timothy,
St Titus 27 St Angela Merici, St Marius 28 St
Amadeus, St Thomas Aquinas, St Peter Thomas;
30 St Hyacintha, St Martina; 31 St Aidan, St Cyrus
and St John of Alexandria, St Francis Xavier.

February

1 St Brid or Brigid of Kildare 2 St Joan 3 St Blaise,
St Laurence of Canterbury, St Margaret of England
4 St Andrew, St Joan 5 St Adelaide, St Agatha
7 St Luke the Younger, St Moses, St Theodore,
St Elfleda, St John, St Benedict, St Lucius
12 St Antony, St Julian, St Marina 13 St Catherine,
St Stephen 14 St Valentine, St John Baptist;
St Abraham 16 St Jeremy, St Gilbert, St Juliana
17 St Finan of Lindisfarne 18 St Colman of
Lindisfarne, St Flavian, St Leo 19 St Conrad;
20 St Wulfric 21 St George Amastris, St Peter
Damian 23 St Alexander Akimetes, St Boswell
25 St Louis 26 St Alexander, St Nestor, St Victor
27 St Gabriel Possenti, St John 28 St Oswald of
Worcester.

Irma (G)
German short form of Irmegard, meaning 'whole'. The
English form is Emma.

Irving (B)
Scottish surname and placename, meaning 'west river'.
Washington Irving (1783–1859) was the creator of Rip Van
Winkle and his father came from Orkney.

Irwin (B)
From Anglo-Saxon 'eoforwine', meaning 'sea's friend'.

Isaac (B)
Latin form of the Greek Isaak, meaning 'laughter'; this was
Sarah's reaction, in the Old Testament, when she heard that
she was pregnant in old age.

Isaak (B)
Greek, meaning 'laughter', the equivalent of the Hebrew
Yitschak, the name of two Byzantine emperors and a
Russian saint.

Isabeau (G)
Oldest form of Isabel which originated in Provence in the south of France in the Middle Ages. The 'beau' was changed to 'belle' at the French court in Paris. Like Elizabeth, from which all forms of Isabel derive, it means 'God's oath'.

Isabel (G)
English form of the French Isabelle which dates from 12th century. Three French princesses by the name of Isabelle married medieval English kings and by the 14th century it was one of the most popular names, often interchanged with Elizabeth, the name from which it originally derived and with which it shares the meaning, 'God's oath'. It has been a great favourite of the 20th century.

Isabella (G)
Spanish and Latin form of Isabel, meaning 'god's oath'.

Isabelle (G)
French form of Isabel which dates from the Middle Ages.

Isadora (G)
From ancient Greek 'isidore', meaning 'gift of Isis'.

Isambard (B)
From Old German, with the associations of iron and giant.

Iseult (G)
Old French form of an ancient Celtic name Essylt meaning 'beautiful to behold'. The story of Tristan and Iseult appears in Welsh, Cornish and Breton legend.

Ishbel (G)
Charming Scottish form of Isabel, meaning 'God's oath'.

Isla (B&G)
Scottish river name, pronounced Eye-la, occasionally bestowed as a Christian name.

Ismay (G)
Pretty medieval name of unknown origin, although it may be a form of the French Esmée, found in Ireland in the 18th century.

Isobel (G)
Scottish spelling of Isabel.

Isolde (G)
Germanic form of Iseult, meaning 'beautiful to behold'. The Italian form is Isota.

Ivan (B)
Russian form of Hebrew John, meaning 'grace of God' and the name of six Russian kings and tsars. It came into use in England in the 19th century when there was a fashion for Russian names.

Ivana (G)
Russian form of the Hebrew Johanna, meaning 'grace of God'.

Ivo (B)
English form of the French Yves, meaning 'well-born'. It was a favourite Anglo-Norman name.

Ivor (B)
English form of the Welsh and Old Breton Ifor, meaning 'lord'.

Ivy (G)
English botanical name, which became fashionable at the end of the 19th century.

J

Jack (B)
From Flemish form of John, meaning 'grace of God'. The pet form of the Flemish Jan was Jankin which passed into English first as Jackin and later as Jack. It was an immensely popular name at the end of the Middle Ages, both as a name in its own right and as an affectionate form of John.

Jacob (B)
From Hebrew 'aqob', meaning 'supplanter'. Jacob, in the Old Testament, was the son of Rebecca and Isaac. His name was revived by the Puritans in the 17th century for its biblical associations and was used interchangeably with James.

Jacqueline (G)
French feminine form of Jacques, or James. It was known in medieval England and in Shakespeare's time, but was then out of fashion until the present century when it became popular for its French feel.

Jacquetta (G)
French Luxembourg form of Jacqueline which was in use in the Middle Ages. A Jaquenetta appears in Shakespeare's *Love's Labour's Lost*.

Jacques (B)
French form of James, from the Greek Jakobus, which dates from the Middle Ages. It is a classic French name.

Jade (G)
Jewel name popularized by Mick Jagger who bestowed it on his daughter. It is now among the top 20 girls' names in Britain.

Jake (B)
English form of the French Jacques which dates from the

early 14th century. It is sometimes used as a short form of Jacob.

James (B)
From Spanish Jaime, which itself came from the Italian Giacomo, meaning 'one who supplants'. The name is Hebrew in origin, from the same stem as Jacob, and was used, in an effort to flatter the monarch James I, to translate the names of the two apostles who appear in the Greek and Latin texts as Jacobus, in the King James version of the Bible of 1611. One of the great Scottish names, its fortunes have been more mixed in England. The 60s, however, saw a revival of interest in New Testament names and James has been in the top ten names since.

Jamie (B)
Scottish affectionate form of James, which dates back to 16th century. James in Scotland was pronounced, and sometimes written, Jeames which suggests that the early pronunciation of Jamie was close to Jim-my.

Jancis (G)
Combination of Jane and Cicely.

Jane (G)
From Hebrew 'johanna', meaning 'grace of God'. The earliest form of Jane was Joan, which was one of the three commonest girls' names in the Middle Ages. The first significant English Jane was Henry VIII's third wife, Jane Seymour. Lady Jane Grey, who was born the year that Jane Seymour died was christened in her memory. The name was in use until the 19th century when it was ousted in favour of Joan by the Victorians. It has become immensely popular again this century, however.

Janet (G)
Diminutive of Jane which dates from the Middle Ages with the association of 'grace of God'. Janeta is found in English medieval records. In Scotland, where the name has long been popular, the affectionate form of Jean was Jennet. It has been popular in the present century as an alternative to Jane.

Eighteenth-century names

The fashion for continental endings in the 18th century brought a new stock of names for girls. While some, such as Sophia and Carolina were influenced by the Hanoverian Royal Family and their Court, others, such as Louisa, Anna, Joanna, Maria and Isabella were more or less home-grown, but made more fashionable by the new continental 'a' ending.

There were also wilder inventions: Georgiana and Angelica were first used among the aristocracy. Pamela was invented and Clarissa resurrected by Samuel Richardson as names for the heroines of his novels. Fanny Burney revived the name Evelina and her novel *Camilla* (1796) made an old name popular again at the font. The royal Saxon name, Emma, obsolete for 600 years was also revived and in Scotland, Patricia, a feminine form of Patrick, appeared for the first time.

Typical 18th-century girls' names:

Angelina, Anna, Belinda, Camilla, Carolina, Cecilia, Evelina, Georgiana, Isabella, Julia, Juliana, Louisa, Maria, Melissa, Olivia, Pamela, Patricia, Sophia

Meanwhile, the stock of boys' names was enriched by the return of some old English names which had been out of use for centuries. The 'Gothic' revival that swept fashionable society towards the end of the century made its impression. Back, after many centuries in the wilderness, came the great Saxon names Edgar, Alfred, Edmond and Edwin.

Some traditional names fell on harder times. In Jane Austen's *Northanger Abbey*, we are told that Catherine Morland's father 'was a very respectable man, though his name was Richard'.

Janetta (G)
Pretty late medieval form of Jane.

Janice (G)
Diminutive of Jane, with the association of 'grace of God', which has become popular since the 50s. An alternative spelling is Janis.

Janine (G)
French diminutive of Jeanne, meaning 'grace of God', also spelt Jeannine. It was the most popular name in France in the 30s.

Jasmine (G)
Persian and Arabic flower name which is also spelt Yasmin.

Jason (B)
Greek name used to translate the Hebrew Joshua. In Greek legend, Jason led the Argonauts in search of the golden fleece.

Jasper (B)
English form of the French Gaspard, meaning 'the treasurer', in biblical legend the name of one of the Three Wise Men.

Jay (B)
English, meaning 'the chatterer', the name given to the jay bird. It is very popular in the United States.

Jayne (G)
Modern form of Jane which has become popular in the 20th century, with the meaning 'grace of God'.

Jean (G)
Scottish form of Jane, originating from the Old French Jehane, which dates from 16th century. The pet form is Jeanie.

Jeanne (G)
French version of the Hebrew 'johanna', meaning 'grace of God', the English form being Jane. The earliest form of Jeanne was the Provençal Jehane which is found in the Middle Ages.

Jeannette (G)
French, literally meaning 'little Jeanne', but with the

association of 'grace of God'. It has been popular in Scotland since the 18th century.

Jeffrey (B)
Alternative spelling of Geffrey or Geoffrey which dates from the late Middle Ages. All versions of the name were out of fashion between the 16th and 19th centuries, but were revived by the Victorians for their Old English feel and courtly associations.

Jem (B)
Short form of James and Jeremy which dates from the 16th century.

Jemima (G)
Hebrew, meaning 'dove' and the name of the eldest of the three beautiful daughters of Job. In use from the 17th century, it became very popular in Victorian times. The correct Hebrew spelling is Jemimah.

Jennifer (G)
Cornish form of the Welsh Guenevere, meaning 'fair'. It has been in more or less continuous use in Cornwall from the Middle Ages and came into general use in England and the United States from the 20s. The pet form is Jinny.

Jeremy (B)
From Hebrew 'jiremejahu', meaning 'rise up and exalt'. It appears in records of the Middle Ages both as Jeremy and Jeremias.

Jerome (B)
From Greek, meaning 'holy name'. St Jerome translated the Bible from Greek into Latin in the fourth century and his name appears in various forms throughout Western Europe: Geronimo in Italy, Jérôme in France and Hieronymus in the Low Countries.

Jerry (B)
Shortened form, much used in the 20th century, of Jeremy, Gerald and Gerard.

Jervis (B)
An English spelling, popular in the Middle Ages, of the French Gervase, the name of a first-century martyr.

Jessamy (G)
Old form of Jasmin or Jasmine which dates from the Middle Ages.

Jesse (B)
Hebrew, meaning 'the Lord is'. Jesse was the father of David, and the House of David was of the 'Stem of Jesse'. It has always been a more popular name in the United States – for example, Jesse Jackson – than in England, but the revival of interest in bibilical names in the 80s has brought it back into usage.

Jessica (G)
Hebrew, meaning 'God is looking'. Until Shakespeare's time, the name was used only by Jews and so, in *The Merchant of Venice*, Jessica is Shylock's daughter. Since the late 80s, Jessica has been in the top ten names for girls.

Jessie (G)
Scottish pet form of Janet which dates from the 18th century. It is also used as an affectionate form of Jessica.

Jesus (B)
A fairly common Christian name in Roman Catholic Spain, in the same way that Mohammed is used in Muslim countries. Jesus never came into use in Protestant Northern Europe.

Jethro (B)
Hebrew, meaning 'abundance'. It was used as a Christian name in the 17th and 18th centuries, but hardly at all since.

Jill (G)
A shortened form of Gillian, but used as a name in its own right this century. It came, like Gillian, from the medieval name, Juliana.

Jim (B)
Shortened form of James which originated in Scotland. Six Scottish kings were called James, but it was written and pronounced Jeames, hence the pet form, Jim. It is a name associated with Lowland Scotland, along with Jimmy.

Joan (G)
From Hebrew 'johanna', meaning 'grace of God'. Joan

arrived in England from the South of France at the time of the Crusades and quickly became one of the three most popular girls' names. It was supplanted by Jane in Shakespeare's time. George Bernard Shaw's *Saint Joan* (1923) sparked a revival of interest.

Joanna (G)
From the Hebrew 'johanna', meaning 'grace of God'. It appears twice in the New Testament but was not used as a Christian name in England until the 17th century when it was popular among Puritans. It was particularly popular in the 50s. Joanne is an alternative.

Jocasta (G)
Greek, with the meaning of 'shining moon'. Jocasta was Queen of Thebes.

Jock (B)
Scottish version of Jack dating from the 18th century.

Jocunda (G)
Latin, meaning 'pleasant'.

Joel (B)
Hebrew, meaning 'the Lord is God'.

Johanna (G)
As the name from which Joanna and Joan are descended, Johanna is the closest to the Hebrew original 'johanna', meaning 'grace of God'. It was very popular in the mid-18th century among the aristocracy and is occasionally found today.

John (B)
One of the great European Christian names, John derives from the Hebrew 'Jochanaan', meaning 'the Lord is gracious' and was popular with both Jews and Christians in biblical times through associations with John the Baptist and John the Evangelist. The name was brought back to England during the Crusades in the 12th century and quickly established itself as a popular and steadfast name. In many ways it is the quintessential English name, a name for all seasons and all centuries and still going strong.

Dear John: the most popular names ever

More Englishmen have been called John, William or Thomas, and more Englishwomen called Elizabeth, Mary or Anne, than any other names in British history. For several centuries one person in two of the population would bear one of these six names! The historian E G Withycombe, whose classic *Dictionary of English Christian Names* was first published in 1945 and is still in print, has shown that at certain times during the last 800 years your chances of not having one of these names were slender indeed. At the end of the 14th century, when Geoffrey Chaucer was writing *The Canterbury Tales*, only 36 per cent of boys weren't called Henry, John, Richard, Robert or William. Equally in the 18th century, four in ten girls were called Elizabeth or Mary, while a quarter of all boys between 1700 and 1749 were called John.

John, of course, has had its detractors. The poet John Keats wrote in a letter to his sister-in-law: ''Tis a bad name and goes against a man. If my name had been Edmund, I should have been more fortunate.' A modern John would seem to agree. John Cleese told the *Daily Telegraph*: 'It's a dreadful name and that is why I am delighted that my wife calls me Jack. Jack is so much racier, Brian is also a much better name. Whoever heard of people getting Dear Jack or Dear Brian letters?'

Jolyon (B)
Thought to be a north of England version of Julian, it was used by John Galsworthy as a family Christian name in his epic *The Forsyte Saga*, with the charming diminutive of Jolly.

Jonathan (B)
Hebrew, meaning 'gift of the Lord'. Jonathan was the son of the King of Saul in the Old Testament. The name

was revived by the Puritans in the 17th century and by the 18th century had come into general use. It declined in the 19th century but has flourished in the present century, particularly since the 50s. An alternative spelling is Jonathon.

Joos (B)
Flemish form of the Breton Joisse, meaning 'champion' and the name from which Joscelyn was derived.

Jordan (B)
From Hebrew, meaning 'flowing down' and the name of the great river in Palestine. It was used as a Christian name from the end of the 12th century when the Crusaders brought back much-prized holy water from the River Jordan. Its sudden popularity in the late 80s and early 90s may be due to the footballer Joe Jordan.

Joscelyn (B&G)
The use of Joscelyn as a girl's name is a 20th-century phenomenon, but as a boy's name it has been in use since the Middle Ages. It was a Breton name, from 'josse' meaning 'champion', and was brought over by the Normans.

Josie (G)
Affectionate form of Josephine which has almost become a name in its own right in the present century.

Joseph (B)
From Hebrew, meaning 'may God add'. It was a popular name in Israel at the time of Christ and, until the Middle Ages in Europe, was a purely Jewish name. In 1621 Joseph of Nazareth, husband of Mary, was given a feast day of 19 March and his name came into general use in both Catholic and Protestant Europe.

Josepha (G)
Pretty feminine form of Joseph which became very popular from the 17th century. The French form was Joséphe.

Josephine (G)
French diminutive of Joséphe which was coined for Marie-Joséphe Rose Tascher de la Pagerie when she became

Napoleon's empress. It was adopted in England in the 19th century for its royal and romantic associations.

Josette (G)
French pet form of Joséphe and Josephine.

Joshua (B)
Hebrew, meaning 'the Lord is generous' and, like Joseph, a popular name among Jews at the time of Christ. It was revived by the Puritans in the 17th century for its biblical associations and has remained in use ever since. It is tipped to become one of the great boys' names of the 90s.

Josiah (B)
Hebrew, meaning 'may the Lord heal' and one of the biblical names revived by the Puritans in the 17th century.

Joy (G)
English, meaning 'joy', one of the names coined by the Puritans in the 17th century.

Joyce (G)
From Breton, with the association of champion. Joisse was the name of a seventh-century saint whose name was rendered in Latin as Jocea and subsequently Joyce in the Middle Ages. It was revived at the end of the 19th century for its medieval and religious associations.

Jude (B)
Greek form of Hebrew Judah, meaning 'praise'.

Judith (G)
Ancient Hebrew, meaning 'woman of Judaea'. The most famous biblical Judith was Judith of Bethulia who saved her countrymen by killing the general, Holofernes. It was revived by the Puritans for its biblical associations and became popular enough to warrant an affectionate form Judy which dates from the start of the 18th century.

Jules (B)
French form of Julian which dates from the 16th century.

Julia (G)
From Italian Giulia, coined by Shakespeare into an English form for one of the women in his play *The Two Gentlemen*

Christmas names

For many centuries children were named according to the religious festivals of the time of year they were born. In Russia Anastasia, meaning 'resurrection', was given to girls born at Easter. Boys born at this time in France were christened Pascal, and in Cornwall Pasco or Pascow.

Modern names suitable for Christmas babies: Natalie, Natalia, Natasha, Natalina (Latin 'natale domini', meaning 'birthday of the Lord' or 'Christmas Day'), Mary (Hebrew Miriam, meaning 'wished for'), Tiffany (traditionally given to girls born during the Epiphany), Emmanuelle (French, meaning 'God with us'), Stella (Latin, meaning 'star'), Holly (English plant name), Noelle (French, meaning 'Christmas'), Carol, Ivy (English plant name), Nollaig (Irish, meaning 'Christmas'), Stephen (the feast of Stephen is 26 December), Nicholas (patron saint of Christmas), Noël (French, meaning 'Christmas'), Dominic (Latin, meaning 'day of the Lord'), Christian (French, meaning 'a Christian'), Caspar (one of the Three Wise Men), Robin (diminutive of Robert), Emanuel (French, meaning 'God with us').

Saints' feast days of the twelve days of Christmas

25 Christmas Day: St Anastasia, St Eugenia
26 Boxing Day: St Stephen 27 St Fabiola, St John the Evangelist 28 St Antony, St Theodore 29 St Thomas of Canterbury 30 St Anysia 31 St Columba, St Melania, St Silvester 1 New Year's Day: St Felix, St Peter, St William 2 St Basil, St Caspar, St Gregory 3 St Genevieve or Genovefa of Paris 4 St Elizabeth Bayley Seton, St Gregory, St Roger 5 St Simeon Stylites

of Verona. It was an immensely popular name in the 17th and 18th centuries and has remained steadily in use in the present century, even experiencing something of a surge in popularity in the last 30 years.

Julian (B)
Latin, originally from the name of a Roman patrician family whose most famous son was Julius Caesar. It came into use at the end of the 19th century when there was a fashion for classical names.

Juliana (G)
From Latin, the name of an early saint whose popularity in the Low Countries has made it a royal name.

Julie (G)
French form of the Italian Giulia which dates from the 16th century. It was popular in the 50s.

Juliet (G)
From Italian Giulietta, meaning 'little Julia', and coined into an English form by Shakespeare for the heroine of *Romeo and Juliet.* Juliette is the more authentic spelling.

June (G)
Name of the sixth month of the year which was coined as a Christian name at the end of the 19th century. Like May and April, it was a popular name in the 30s.

Justin (B)
From Latin 'justus' meaning 'just' or 'fair', and in the form Justinian, the name of two Byzantine emperors. It came into use in England at the end of the 19th century when classical names were popular.

Justine (G)
French form of Justin, meaning 'just' or 'fair' which was popularized by Lawrence Durrell's famous *Alexandria Quartet* of the 50s. The earliest record of the name being used in England was as Justina, a Justina Humphrey being christened in 1556 and named in honour of St Justina of Padua.

K

Karen (G)
Danish form of Katharine, meaning 'pure'. It was taken to the United States by Danish immigrants in the 19th century and has been a popular name since the 50s. An alternative spelling is Karin.

Karl (B)
Old German 'kerl', meaning 'a man'. The German and Scandinavian form of Charles which dates from the eighth century.

Kasia (G)
Polish form of Katherine, meaning 'pure' and pronounced Kash-a.

Kate (G)
Short form of Katharine and Katherine which dates from Tudor times.

Katerina (G)
Early Latin form of Katharine. It passed into Italian as Caterina.

Katharine (G)
Greek 'katharos', meaning 'pure'. The first significant bearer was St Katharine of Alexandria who in 310 was put to death on a catherine wheel. Her tomb is on Mount Sinai. Her name was brought back to Western Europe by the Crusaders, who were greatly taken by her story, and has been in continuous use for the last 800 years.

Katherine (G)
Greek Aikaterine, the earliest Greek spelling of the name before it took on the meaning 'katharos' or 'pure'. The Russian Ekaterina is the form of Katherine closest to the original. Katherine is the favoured English spelling.

Kathleen (G)
Irish form of Katherine. The Old French form of Katherine was Cateline, which passed into medieval usage as Catlin. It is from this that Kathleen is derived.

Katie (G)
Pet form of Katharine and Katherine which dates from the end of the last century. Katy is the American spelling.

Katinka (G)
Affectionate form of Ekaterina, the Russian form of Katherine, sometimes used in England as a name in its own right.

Katya (G)
Short form of Ekaterina, the Russian form of Katherine.

Kay (G)
Short form of Katharine coined in the 20th century.

Kayleigh (G)
Blend of Kay and Leigh which is very popular in Scotland at the moment.

Keane (B)
Manx, meaning 'warrior'.

Kegan (B)
Irish surname, sometimes used as a Christian name, meaning 'son of Egan'.

Keith (B)
Originally from Gaelic, meaning 'a woody place'. The earls of Kintore's family seat was Keith Hall and they adopted the name as a family font name. It came into general use in the 30s for its Scottish associations.

Kelly (G)
Irish surname which was first used as a Christian name in the United States in the 50s.

Kelvin (B)
From Anglo-Saxon, meaning 'friend of the ship'.

Kenelm (B)
Old English 'cenhelm', with the associations of bravery and helmet, suggesting that it was a warrior name. Cenhelm, King of Mercia, was a saint-king and his name was revived in the 19th century for its religious and historical feel.

Old Testament names

'For, as his name is, so is he', is written in the Book of Samuel. Over 1,600 people are mentioned by name in the Old Testament, of which 1,500 are men and just a hundred and twenty five are women, and their names are remarkably descriptive of their characters and circumstances.

Many Old Testament names have long and distinguished usage which dates back, if not to medieval times, then certainly to the Reformation and early 17th century when names such as Benjamin, Daniel, Jonathan, Samuel, Joshua, Deborah, Judith, Hannah, Sarah, and Rachel came into popular use. In the second half of the 20th century there has been a revival of interest in biblical names although initially this was confined to the New Testament and names such as Mark, Matthew, Simon, Peter, Paul, James and Timothy, all of which became immensely popular after the Second World War. It was the 80s before the Old Testament names began emerging in force: Daniel, David, Samuel, Rebecca, Jessica, Sarah and Hannah are all in the top ten while Aaron, Joshua, Benjamin and Leah look set to 'climb' as the 1990s progress.

Boys

Aaron 'high mountain'
Abraham 'father of the multitude'
Abram 'father is exalted'
Adam 'red earth'
Alon 'tree of life'
Amos 'burden bearer'
Ariel 'lion of God'
Asa 'physician'
Benjamin 'son of the right hand'
Caleb 'dog' (with the associations of loyalty)
Cyrus Persian 'throne'
Daniel 'God is judge'
Darius Persian 'king'
David 'darling'
Eli 'exalted'
Ethan 'permanent'
Gabriel 'strong man of God'
Hiram 'exalted brother'
Isaac 'laughter'

Jacob 'supplanter'
Jeshua 'salvation'
Jesse 'the Lord is'
Joel 'Lord is God
Jonathan 'gift of the Lord'
Joseph 'may God add'
Joshua 'Lord is salvation'
Malcam 'their king'
Michael 'who is like God'
Moses Egyptian 'child of the Nile'
Nathan 'gift'
Nathaniel 'gift of God'

Nimrod 'rebellious'
Noah 'long-lived'
Omar 'speaker'
Samson 'son'
Samuel 'God has heard'
Saul 'asked-for'
Seth 'compensation'
Simeon 'God has heard'
Solomon 'man of peace'
Tobiah 'God is good'
Uriel 'God is my light'
Zachary 'God remembers'

Girls

Abigail 'a father's joy'
Bathsheba 'daughter of an oath'
Bathshua 'daughter of wealth'
Deborah 'bee '
Delilah 'delight'
Dinah 'judged'
Elisheba 'God is my oath'
Esther Persian 'star'
Eve 'life'
Hannah 'favoured by God'
Hephsibar 'my delight is in her'
Jemimah 'dove'
Jezebel 'chaste'

Judith 'woman of Judah'
Kerenhappuch 'horn of paint'
Keturah 'perfumed'
Keziah 'cassia'
Leah 'cow'
Mehetabel 'God does good'
Miriam 'bitterness'
Naomi 'pleasant'
Rachel 'ewe'
Rebekah 'heifer'
Ruth 'friend'
Sarah 'princess'
Sheerah 'kinswoman'
Shua 'wealth'
Tamar 'date palm'
Vashti (Persian) 'the best'

Kenneth (B)

English form of the Gaelic Cinaed, meaning 'handsome' and the name of the first king of Scotland, Kenneth MacAlpine, who died in 860. Sir Walter Scott brought it into English use in the form of Sir Kenneth, the crusading hero of *The Talisman* (1825).

Keren

Short form of the Hebrew Kerenhappuch, one of the beautiful daughters of Job (the others being Jemimah and Keziah). It was adopted by the Puritans in the 17th century.

Kerensa (G)

Cornish, meaning 'love'.

Kerry (B&G)

Irish county name adopted as a Christian name among the Irish Catholics of Boston in the 19th century. It has also been used as a Christian name in Australia since the 50s.

Keturah (G)

Hebrew, meaning 'fragrance' or 'incense'. Keturah was the 2nd wife of Abraham.

Kevin (B)

From Old Irish, meaning 'handsome by birth', or 'comely' and the name of a sixth-century Irish saint who founded a monastery near Dublin. In the present century, there was a famous Irish nationalist song of 1916 called 'Kevin Barry' and since the 50s it has been a favourite name. One in 20 boys is now named Kevin in France and it is in the top ten in Germany.

Keziah (G)

Hebrew, meaning 'cassia', a bush admired for its fragrance, and one of the three beautiful daughters of Job (the others being Kerenhappuch and Jemimah). It was adopted by the Puritans for its biblical associations and was popular with the Wesleyans in the 18th century, pronounced in the English fashion, Kez-eye-ar.

Kieran (B)

From Irish, meaning 'black-haired'.

Kim (B)
Short form of Kimball, coined by Rudyard Kipling for his novel *Kim* (1901), the story of a little English boy who turns spy in India. It was Harold Adrian Russell Philby's favourite book when he was growing up in India and as an adult he assumed it as his real name. It was the one give-away of his double life as a Russian agent, but the significance of this simple deceit, which must have pleased him greatly, was never grasped.

Kimberley (G)
South African, a name adopted by British soldiers for their daughters born while garrisoned at Kimberley, the South African diamond town, during the Boer War. Since the 50s it has been popular in England, Australia, the United States and South Africa. The short form is Kim.

Kirsten (G)
Scandinavian form of Christiana, meaning 'of the Christian faith', sometimes used in England following the fame of the great opera diva, Kirsten Flagstad.

Kirsty (G)
Scottish pet form of Christiana, which was written Kristyan in the Middle Ages in Scotland. It means 'of the Christian faith'. Kirsty has been used as a name in its own right from the 17th century.

Kit (B)
Short form of Christopher dating at least from the 16th century.

Kitty (G)
Affectionate form of Katharine which dates from the Middle Ages and was often used as a name in its own right until the mid-17th century. It dropped from popularity but was revived at the end of the 19th century.

Knud (B)
Danish, meaning 'knot' and pronounced K-nuth. It is an immensely popular Scandinavian name and long associated with royalty.

Nineteenth-century names

The age of Empire, romanticism, war waged on foreign soil and wedding cake Gothic architecture was unlikely to be retiring in its choice of Christian names. The turnover was rapid, every ten years or so producing new favourites according to the passions and interests of the day. Characters in the novels of Sir Walter Scott (Rowena, Quentin, Amy, Allan, Oliver, Guy, Edmund, Nigel and Wilfred); the heroes and heroines in the poetry of Byron, Wordsworth, Browning (Leila, Pippa, Beatrice and Lucy); names evoking the medievalism of Tennyson and the pre-Raphaelites (Lancelot, Edgar, Winifred, Walter, Arthur, Roger, Joyce, Alice, Gillian, Mavis and Edith); the Tractarian movement's revival of saints' names (Aidan, Ninian and Bede) and jewel names (Topaz, Pearl, Beryl and Ruby); flower names (Violet, Rose, Lily, Ivy, Heather, Holly, Lavender and Marigold); place names (Alma, Florence and Candia); heroic names (Gordon, Clive, Baden and Stanley); and, towards the end of the century, a revival of classical names (Horace, Cecil, Iolanthe, Phyllis and Dorothy).

Interestingly, for a God-fearing age, biblical names were little in demand, except for those names – Samuel and Benjamin, Mary and Elizabeth – which were by then so long woven into the fabric of English nomenclature that their religious association was almost lost. Dickens is the best cataloguer of nonconformist names in the 19th century: Josiah Boundary (*Hard Times*), Soloman Gills (*Dombey and Son*), Barnaby Rudge and Silas Wegg (*Our Mutual Friend*). Aspiring middle-class parents wanted something quite different; their daughters would have the grace and beauty of romantic heroines and their sons the stout hearts of battle heroes and the chivalry of medieval troubadours. Tall orders.

Kyle (B)

Scottish surname deriving from the Water of Coyle in Strathclyde. It came into use as a Christian name in the United States in the 19th century and in recent years has come into use in England.

Kylie (G)

Western Aboriginal, meaning 'boomerang'.

L

Lachlan (B)
From Gaelic 'laochail', meaning 'warlike'. It has traditionally been used in the McLean family and has long been popular in Australia on account of General Lachlan Macquarie, the much-loved Governor of New South Wales 1809–21.

Lalita (G)
Hindu, meaning 'pleasing'.

Lalla (G)
Scottish, meaning 'lowlands dweller'. An alternative is Lally.

Lamorna (G)
Cornish, associated with Lamorna Cove.

Lana (G)
Short form of Irish Alana, meaning 'fair and beautiful' and popularized by Lana Turner.

Lance (B)
From Old French, meaning 'land', suggesting it was a noble and aristocratic name. The diminutive is Lancelot.

Larissa (G)
Greek, meaning 'cheerful'. It was revived at the end of the 19th century when there was a fashion for classical names. The pet form is Lara.

Lark (G)
English bird name, like the French Merle, meaning 'blackbird', which is tipped for the 90s.

Larry (B)
Irish short form of Laurence. The Scottish form, which predates it, is Laurie.

Laura (G)

Medieval Italian, meaning 'laurel', laurel leaves being associated in ancient Rome with victory and poetic inspiration. It was a popular literary and poetic name of the late Middle Ages and 16th century but fell out of use until the 19th century when it was brought back in the fashion for Italian names.

Lauren (G)

Medieval form of Laura, which has become popular again in the 20th century through the association with Lauren Bacall. It is currently in the top ten most popular names.

Laurence (B)

From Latin 'laurentius', meaning 'from the city of laurels', laurels being associated with victory and inspiration in ancient Rome. St Laurence was an important third-century archdeacon of Rome and his feast day is 10 August. His name was immensely popular in the Middle Ages and continued more or less in use until the 19th century when it was handsomely revived for its classical associations.

Lavender (G)

English flower names which came into use at the end of the 19th century.

Lavinia (G)

From Latin, meaning 'from Lavinium', an area which was south of Rome. As the bride of the Trojan hero Aeneas, her name was celebrated in the poetry of the Renaissance.

Lawrence (B)

Late medieval English spelling of Laurence.

Leah (G)

From Hebrew, meaning 'heifer'. In the Old Testament Leah is the sister of Rachel and the wife of Jacob. The name also appears in Arabic.

Lee (B & G)

American surname which came to be used as a Christian name in the Southern states in honour of the confederate general Robert E. Lee (1807–70). The actress Lee Remick was actually christened Ann Remick.

Leeanne(G)
Modern English form of the French Lianne which is rapidly becoming a 90s' name.

Leigh (B)
English spelling of the American Lee.

Leila (G)
Persian, meaning 'dark as night', the love tale of *Leila and Mejnoun* being a classic of Middle Eastern literature. The name was brought into usage in English when Byron chose it for the heroine of his oriental poem 'The Giaour'. An alternative spelling is Leyla.

Lena (G)
German short form of Magdalena, meaning and often used as a name in its own right. Another form is Leni.

Leo (B)
Latin form of Greek 'leon', meaning 'lion' and the name of six emperors of Constantinople and 13 popes. Although found in 13th-century records, it was hardly in use in England until the end of the 19th century when there was a popular revival of classical names.

Leon (B)
Greek, meaning 'lion'.

Leonard (B)
From Frankish, meaning 'as brave as a lion'. There was a sixth-century Frankish saint called St Leonhard and his name was popular in England in the Middle Ages, and also in Italy where he was known as Leonardo. Leonard was revived at the end of the 19th century for its Italian associations.

Leonie (G)
French feminine form of Leon, meaning 'lion'. A more formal version is Leontyne.

Leonora (G)
Italian short form of Eleanora, meaning 'the bright one'. It came into use in England in the mid-19th century when there was a fashion for Italian names and has more or less remained in use since.

Leopold (B)
Ancient Austrian name with the associations of 'fearlessness' and 'people'. It was the name of seven rulers of Austria before 1400 and subsequently of two emperors. Many centuries later, Queen Victoria, whose favourite Uncle Leopold was King of the Belgians, named her third son after him.

Leroy (B)
Old French, meaning 'servant of the king'. It corresponds to Elroy.

Lesley (G)
Scottish feminine form of Leslie which came into use in the 18th century. Robbie Burns' poem 'Bonny Lesley' brought the name to a wider audience, but its real popularity has been in the present century and particularly since the 50s.

Leslie (B)
Distinguished Scottish family surname which was generally adopted as a Christian name in the 19th century for its aristocratic associations.

Lester (B)
Contracted spelling of Leicester, meaning 'dwelling on the River Legra', which has been in use as a Christian name for the last century.

Letitia (G)
From Latin 'laetitia', meaning 'joy'. The Italian form is Letizia.

Lettice (G)
Short form of Letitia, meaning 'joy' which dates back to the Middle Ages. Lettice Knollys was the wife of Robert Devereux, Earl of Essex, Queen Elizabeth's favourite. It was revived, to a certain extent, at the end of the 19th century for its medieval feel.

Letty (G)
Affectionate form of Lettice and Letitia, with the association of joy.

Lewanna (G)
Hebrew, meaning 'moon'.

Lewis (B)
English form of French Louis, which itself derived from a royal Frankish name Clovis meaning 'renowned warrior'. The name came to England with the Normans and was common in the Middle Ages and 16th century. Chaucer called his son Lewis. It was revived at the end of the 19th century for its royal and medieval feel.

Lexy (G)
Affectionate form of Alexandra.

Liam (B)
Irish form of William, meaning 'strong protector'. For many years confined to Ireland, it has recently come into English usage and is tipped to become one of the names of the 90s.

Liane (G)
French, from the Provençal Eliane, meaning 'to bind'. An Old French name, it has come into use in England in the last 30 years.

Libby (G)
Scottish pet form of Elizabeth.

Lilac (G)
Flower name coined in the 19th century as a girl's name.

Lilian (G)
English, associated with the lily flower and in use in Shakespearean England. It was a favourite Victorian and Edwardian christening name. An alternative spelling is Lillian.

Lilibet (G)
Cornish pet form of Elizabeth, which was also the childhood name of Queen Elizabeth II.

Lily (G)
English flower name, with the association of 'purity'. In Christian legend, lilies were the flowers that grew in the places that Eve's tears fell as she left Paradise.

Linda (G)
Spanish, meaning 'pretty'.

Geographical names

In the ancient world people were often known by the town, city or province from which they came and some of these names have become Christian names in their own right. Lydia, for example, derives from the name of a district of Asia Minor. Luke means 'a man from Luciana', Madeleine, 'woman of Magdala', all of which appear in the New Testament. The Romans added Sebastian, Adrian, Maurice, Frances, Lavinia, Roma, and Laurence, derived from place names within the Roman Empire, while Candia, Delia, Cynthia and Rhoda belong to ancient Greece.

The Normans bequeathed aristocratic surnames such as Neville, Percy, Bruce and Darcy, names which had originally indicated the areas of Normandy from which the bearer came. While in Scotland both place names – Gordon (Berwickshire), Leslie (Fife) and Keith (Grampian) and ancient Gaelic descriptive names such as Douglas (from 'dubh glas' meaning 'dark water') and Ailsa (from old Gaelic 'aill' meaning 'a rock') have added to the name stock. Yorkshire has produced two names in this genre, Shirley and Beverley, both used initially for boys, but in the present century better known as girl's names.

Meanwhile, 20th-century parents have shown a preference for the romantic and far-flung. Kerry, Tara, Erin and Clodagh are Irish place and river names and favourites of the ex-patriate Irish communities in America and Australia. India, China and Georgia reflect broader travel horizons and names such as Chelsea, Iona and Skye national affections.

Lindsay (B&G)

Scottish surname which came into use as a Christian name for boys in the 19th century for its Scottish aristocratic feel. Since the 40s it has also become a popular girl's name, often spelt Lindsey.

Lionel (B)

Medieval French, meaning 'young lion' and a name associated with chivalry and courtly love. It became a medieval royal name and was revived in Victorian times for its historical feel. It has declined in popularity in the present century.

Lisa (G)

Short form of Elizabeth, in use since the 50s.

Livia (G)

Roman family name, of which the best known female member was the wife of Emperor Claudius.

Lizzy (G)

Affectionate form of Elizabeth, also spelt Lizzie, which has been in use for at least 200 years. Elizabeth Bennet in Jane Austen's *Pride and Prejudice* (1813) is known as Lizzy.

Lloyd (B)

Old Welsh 'lluyd', meaning 'grey-haired'. It was a surname which came into use as a Christian name in the mid-20th century.

Lodovico (B)

Italian form of Louis used by Shakespeare in *Othello*.

Lois (G)

From Greek, pronounced 'Low-iss'. In the New Testament she is the grandmother of Timothy. It was favoured by the Puritans and taken to the United States, where it has remained popular, particular in New England.

Lola (G)

Spanish pet form of Dolores, meaning 'sorrows'. Dolores became associated with Hollywood in the 30s. The diminutive is Lolita.

Lora (G)

Provençal spelling of the Italian Laura, meaning 'laurel'. Lora de Sades of Avignon was the inspiration for much of the work of the 14th-century Italian poet, Petrarch.

Loretta (G)
Literally 'little Lora', from the Provençal name for Laura.

Lorin (B)
Austrian and German form of Laurence.

Lorna (G)
Invented by R D Blackmore for the heroine of his novel *Lorna Doone* (1869), it has become popular in this century.

Lorraine (G)
Region of France which became a Christian name in the early years of the century. George Bernard Shaw's play *Saint Joan* may have brought the name to public attention, since in it she is described as the Maid of Lorraine as well as of Orleans. It was a popular name in the 50s and 60s.

Louis (B)
French, with the associations of 'glory' and 'fight', the name of 18 French kings and the quintessential regal name. It was introduced here by the Normans but pronounced Loo-is, which in time led to the English spelling of Lewis.

Louisa (G)
Latin form of the French Louise which dates from the 18th century. Jane Austen had a Louisa in her novel *Persuasion* (1818), indicating that it was in regular use.

Louise (G)
French feminine form of Louis introduced to England in the 17th century. An early spelling was Luese. Its French origins made it popular with romantic novelists in the 19th century and it has survived well into present times.

Loulou (G)
French affectionate form of Louise.

Lucas (B)
Originally from Greek, meaning 'man of Lucania' and the earliest form of Luke known in England.

Lucette (G)
French diminutive of Lucy, meaning 'light', sometimes found in England in the Middle Ages.

Lucia (G)
From Latin, meaning 'light'. The name was given to girls born at daybreak and was popularized by St Lucia of Sicily. The modern Italian form is also Lucia, pronounced Loo-chee-ah.

Lucian (B)
From Latin, and the name of two early saints both of whom were natives of Syria. It occurs as a Christian name in the 12th and 13th centuries but more or less fell into disuse in later centuries. Revived at the end of the 19th century, it came to be regarded as an attractive alternative to Luke. The French form is Lucien.

Lucilla (G)
From Latin, meaning 'light'. An imperial name, borne by several Roman empresses. St Lucilla was a third-century Roman martyr.

Lucille (G)
French form of Lucilla.

Lucinda (G)
Poetic and literary version of Lucy, meaning 'light' coined in the 17th century and popular in the 18th. It has been revived in the 20th century.

Lucretia (G)
Feminine form of Lucretius and the name of a celebrated Roman beauty. It was a fairly common name in the north of England from the 16th to 18th centuries. The Italian form is Lucrezia.

Lucy (G)
From Latin 'lux', meaning 'light' and traditionally given to girls born at daybreak. Introduced by the Normans, an early form was Luce, although this was probably pro-nounced as Lucy. It became a favourite Victorian name because of Wordsworth's 'Lucy' poems. Shakespeare also uses the variations Luciana and Lucetta.

Ludmilla (G)
Russian and Slavic, meaning 'beloved of the people'.

Ludovic (B)

From Ludovicus, the Latin form of the Frankish royal name Clovis. It has been a favourite name in the Highlands since the 17th century. The Italian form is Ludovico. Ludowick and Ludwig are German.

Ludovica (G)

Feminine form of Ludovic which is sometimes used in Scotland and Ireland.

Luisa (G)

Italian form of Louise, meaning 'famous in war'.

Luke (B)

From Greek Loukas, meaning 'someone from Lucania'. St Luke was the author of the third gospel and was a doctor, painter and writer. His symbol was the ox, which was associated with patience. The Puritans popularized his name in the 17th century and it has been in regular use in the United States since that time. It shot to popularity during the 80s and has since stayed in the top ten.

Lulu (G)

Pet form of Lucy and Louise.

Lydia (G)

From Greek, meaning 'woman from Lydia'. Lydia was a district of Asia Minor in biblical times and the Lydians were supremely talented, inventing coinage and famed as musicians. A Lydia is mentioned in the New Testament and for this reason it became a favourite name with the Puritans. By the 18th century it had become associated with lazy society beauties epitomized by Oliver Goldsmith's Lydia Languish in *She Stoops to Conquer*. The Slavic form is Lidija.

Lyn (G)

From Welsh Eiluned (pronounced Eli-ned), meaning 'idol'. The Old French form of Eiluned was Linet, suggesting that the two names were linked by a common Celtic heritage.

Lynette (G)

Anglicized version of the Old Welsh and French Eiluned or Linet, popularized by Tennyson in his bestselling tale of 'Gareth and Lynette' published in 1872.

Medieval style

The present century has been equalled only by the 12th century for the breadth and range of names used by parents to name their children, many of which are surprising for their apparent modernity. Among the Williams, Johns and Thomases, it was not unusual to come across Colins, Lukes, Jordans, Daniels, Patricks, Michaels, Martins, Jonathans and Simons, names which then disappeared at the end of the Middle Ages and often did not reappear until our own century.

The pool of names for girls was even wider. Emma, Camilla, Grace, Isabel, Sara, Lucy, Laura and Katherine were all medieval names, along with Anastasia, Jacqueline, Tiffany, Colette, Cassandra and Christina. For India and Florence, read the 12th-century equivalents: Grecia, Italia, Paris and Pavia.

Medieval names

Boys	Hilary	Philip
Adrian	Jacob	Robin
Antony	James	Silvester
Benedict	Jeremy	Simon
Brian	Jonathan	
Brice	Jordan	
Charles	Leon	
Christopher	Leonard	*Girls*
Clem	Lewis	Agatha
Colin	Lionel	Agnes
Constantine	Lucas	Alice
Crispin	Luke	Aline
Daniel	Marcus	Anastasia
Denis	Mark	Ann
Felix	Martin	Annabel
George	Michael	Anne
Giles	Patrick	Antigone
Gregory	Paul	Beatrice

Cassandra	Jacqueline	Marion
Cecily	Janet	Mary
Christina	Joan	Mirabel
Clare	Joy	Muriel
Clarissa	Joyce	Olive
Colette	Kate	Ottilie
Constance	Katherine	Petronella
Eleanor	Laura	Philippa
Elizabeth	Lavinia	Rosa
Emma	Lettice	Rosamond
Eve	Lucia	Sabina
Felicity	Madeline	Sara
Gillian	Margaret	Susanna
Grace	Margery	Sybil
Honor	Maria	Tiffany

Lynn (G)
From modern French Lynnette, associated with the Welsh
Eiluned, meaning 'idol'.

Lys (G)
Royal French flower name. Lys, pronounced Lee or Lee-se,
is the lily of the royal French emblem, the fleur-de-lys.

Lysander (B)
From Greek, meaning 'liberator of men'. The name of a
great Greek hero and one of Shakepeare's youthful lovers
in *A Midsummer Night's Dream*.

Lysanne (G)
Modern combination of Elizabeth and Anne.

M

Mabs (G)
Affectionate name for Mabel and sometimes Mary. Queen Mab appears in folk legend as a mischievous queen of the fairies and Shakespeare uses her in this guise in *A Midsummer Night's Dream.*

Mabel (G)
From Latin 'amabilis', meaning 'lovable'. It first appeared as Anabel or Mabella in the Middle Ages and was a favourite north of England and Victorian name.

Madeleine (G)
French form of the Hebrew Magdalen, meaning 'woman of Magdala'. A favourite from the 16th century in France, from where it came to England, but did not properly establish itself until the present century.

Madeline (G)
English form of French Madeleine, ith short form Maddy.

Madge (G)
Short form of Margaret which dates as a name in its own right from the 16th century. It was especially popular in the 19th century.

Madlin (G)
Welsh form of Madeleine, or Magdalen.

Madoc (B)
Welsh, meaning 'fortunate', also spelt Madog. The English version is Madox.

Mae (G)
American form of May, popularized by Mae West.

Maeve (G)
From Old Irish 'Meadhbh', meaning 'joy'. Meadhbh was a mischievous fairy of Irish legend, known in English as

Queen Mab, who rides her chariot over sleeping people and brings on dreams.

Magda (G)
German short form of Magdalen.

Magdalen (G)
Hebrew, meaning 'woman of Magdala'. Mary Magdalen was one of the women who tended Christ after the crucifixion. It was a popular medieval name but was largely replaced by Madeleine at the Reformation. The short form is Maddy.

Maggie (G)
Scottish pet form of Margaret, dating from the 16th century.

Magnus (B)
Latin, meaning 'great' and a royal name first adopted by Magnus, King of Norway and Denmark in the 11th century who mistook it as the real name of Carolus Magnus, or Charlemagne, rather than as a description, Charles the Great. The name of a number of Scandinavian kings, popular in Iceland, Scotland and the Shetland Islands.

Maidie (G)
Scottish pet form of Margaret.

Máire (G)
Irish form of Mary or Marie, pronounced Moi-re. It was considered too sacred for use in Ireland until the mid-17th century, but has since been immensely popular. This century, one in four girls in Ireland have been named Máire or Mary.

Mairin (G)
Irish, a diminutive of Máire, pronounced Moy-reen.

Maisie (G)
Scottish affectionate form of Margaret.

Malachy (B)
Hebrew, meaning 'messenger'.

Malati (G)
Hindu, meaning 'vine'.

Twentieth-century names

No century has been better documented in the naming of its children than the 20th century, nor has the turnover of popular names been greater or parents more restless in their pursuit of original names for their offspring. Better documentation is the result of improved birth records at Somerset House. (Civil registration began in England and Wales in 1837.) Changes in fashion reflect the changes of the century – two World Wars, the speed of technological advances, cinema, television and, curiously, nostalgia: names, like twins, skip a generation or two. All in all, it's a sociologist's dream of aspirations and preoccupations, collective public imagination and unconsciously revealed attitudes to monarchy, religion and patriotism.

Edwardian parents were traditional in the naming of their children: English kings' names were popular (Edward, Henry, George, John, William, Charles, James and Alfred), as were medieval names (Harold, Walter, Edgar, Percy and Edwin) and classical names (Cecil, Cyril and Hector). Biblical names were supplanted by names of a strong patriotic and royalist nature. Daughters were still christened in the late-Victorian manner; flower names, including Rose, Daisy and Marigold, classical Greek names, such as Dorothy, Doris, Dora and Phyllis and medieval names like Edith, Lilian, Beatrice, Ellen and Alice were all extremely popular.

After the First World War, names with patriotic or monarchical associations began to fall into decline. In their place, in the 20s were the romantic names of the Celtic renaissance (Ronald, Dennis, Kenneth, Douglas, Donald, Brian, Gerald, Alan, Derek, Kathleen, Eileen, Gladys, Gwen, Sheila, Doreen and Deirdre) and medieval names with chivalric associations (Joan, Joyce, Audrey, Arthur and Geoffrey). Biblical names were still rare, although Thomas and John had long been in use. Peter made its first appearance.

Royal and traditional English names continued to wane during the Second World War and in the postwar era. For the first time in 400 years, there was a flood of boys' names with biblical associations: David, Michael, Peter, Paul, Stephen, Philip, James, Andrew and Christopher. The pool of names with Celtic associations also increased to include Colin, Graham, Keith, Nigel and Neil, and in the 50s, Trevor and Barry. Girls' names were affected differently after the war, returning soldiers introducing French names (Valerie, Pauline, Natalie, Yvonne, Jacqueline and Denise). The imitation of the more relaxed American habit of naming children also gave rise to distinctive 50s' favourites (Susan, Carol, Sandra, Lesley, Lynne, Helen, Christine, Wendy, Angela and Shirley).

The 80s brought a minor revolution in names. A study of 180,000 children who were members of a book club produced a list of the ten most popular names for boys and girls: James, Matthew, Christopher, Thomas, David, Daniel, Andrew, Michael, Richard and Jonathan for boys; and Sarah, Laura, Emma, Rebecca, Hannah, Rachel, Katie, Amy, Charlotte and Claire for girls. As the decade wore on, there was a slight shift away from names with biblical associations towards traditional English names like Henry, Edward, William, Elizabeth, Alice, Catherine and Eleanor. James, Thomas, Alexander, Emily, Sophie and Sarah appeared with most frequency in *The Times* birth columns. The most distinctive 80s' names were Luke (replacing Mark) and Rebecca (with its new spelling, Rebekah).

Malcolm (B)
English form of the Gaelic 'mael columb', meaning 'servant of Colm' in reference to St Columba or St Colm of Iona. It was a royal name, the name of four early Scottish kings. It was adopted for general use in the late 19th century for its historical and Scottish associations.

Malise (B)
English form of the Gaelic 'mael Iosa', meaning 'servant of Jesus'.

Manfred (B)
From Old German, meaning 'man of peace' and brought to England by the Normans and revived in the 19th century.

Manon (G)
French diminutive of Marie, popularized by Puccini's opera *Manon Lescaut*. An alternative form is Minette.

Manley (B)
English surname sometimes used as a Christian name.

Marc (B)
French form of Mark, derived from the Latin Marcus. It is popular in Scotland.

Marcel (B)
French, meaning 'little Marc'; Italian form is Marcello.

Marcella (G)
Italian feminine form of Marcello, its diminutive being Marcellina.

Marcia (G)
The feminine form of Marcus, meaning 'warlike'. An early-18th-century literary name, long associated with Scotland.

Marco (B)
Venetian, meaning 'warlike'. It is said that at any point in the last 1,000 years, one Venetian boy in five bore the name of Venice's patron saint and guardian angel.

Marcus (B)
Roman, meaning 'warlike', Marcus Antonius, or Mark Antony, being its most famous bearer.

Margaret (G)

From Persian, meaning 'child of light'. It passed into Greek as Margaretes and was in use in biblical times. Princess Margarete of Hungary married into the royal house of Scotland in 1069 and established the name in the British Isles. Although out of fashion between the 16th and 18th centuries, it has generally maintained its position as one of the top five most popular names of all time.

Margareta (G)

Medieval Latin spelling of Margaret still used today.

Margery (G)

Old English name may have developed from Margaret or as a name associated with the herb, marjoram. Either way it was known in the 16th century and the poet Tennyson revived it in the last century.

Margherita (G)

Charming Italian form of Margaret which has also given rise to Rita. Rita Hayworth was originally named Margarita Cansino.

Margot (G)

French diminutive of Marguerite, meaning 'little child of light'.

Marguerite (G)

Old French form of Margaret, meaning 'child of light', which was established in France in the 16th century. As well as its Persian and Greek associations, it is also a flower name. Marguerite is French for daisy.

Mari (G)

Scottish form of Marie, pronounced, distinctively Maar-ree.

Maria (G)

Latin and Spanish form of Mary, meaning 'wished-for'. It was adopted by the aristocracy in the 18th century, pronounced Mar-eye-ah and became associated with society beauties and literary heroines. In the 20th century the usual pronunciation has been Mar-ee-ah.

Marianne (G)

French, coined in the 18th century from Marie and Anne.

In France Marianne is the personification of the French Republic, in the way that Britannia symbolizes England and her sculptural likeness, modelled by such people as Catherine Deneuve, Brigitte Bardot and latterly Ines de la Fressange, adorns all town halls. The name was popularized through Tennyson's poem 'Mariana' (1830) and has remained in more or less constant use since.

Marie (G)
French form of Maria, meaning 'wished-for'. It has been particularly popular since the 50s.

Mariel (G)
Bavarian diminutive of Mary, meaning 'wished-for'. The Italian form is Mariella.

Mariette (G)
French diminutive of Marie, popularized in England by H E Bates's *The Darling Buds of May* (1958).

Marigold (G)
English, one of the flower names which came into use at the turn of the century.

Marilyn (G)
Combination of English Mary and Welsh Lyn which was coined in the 20th century. It has become popular since the 50s, mainly through its association with Marilyn Monroe.

Marina (G)
From Latin, meaning 'of the sea'. St Marina of Alexandria was an early saint and her name passed into the Greek Orthodox Church. It first came into use in England in the 30s following the marriage of Princess Marina of Greece to Prince George of Kent.

Marion (G)
One of the medieval diminutives of Mary which came to renewed popularity in the 19th century and which has remained a great 20th-century favourite. An alternative spelling is Marian.

Marius (B)
Roman patrician name, probably associated with the Roman god of war Mars which was revived for its classical feel at the end of the 19th century.

Aramaic names

A small group of names are Aramaic in origin, Aramaic being the official language of the Persian Empire from the eighth century BC and the everyday language of Palestine at the time of Christ which was spoken, in all likelihood, by him and the apostles. It is a Semitic language, that is part of the group of languages of the Middle East and North Africa of which the living languages are Hebrew, Arabic and Maltese, and is in use, some 2,000 years later, in Lebanese villages.

Barnabas, meaning 'son of exhortation'
Ira, meaning 'the stallion' and the name of a priest of David
Martha, meaning 'lord'
Mehetabel, meaning 'God is active'
Salome, meaning 'peace of Zion'
Samantha, meaning 'listener'
Tabitha, meaning 'gazelle'
Thomas, meaning 'twin'

Marjorie (G)
Scottish affectionate form of Margaret which had established itself as a name in its own right by the 12th century. Robert the Bruce called his daughter Marjorie.

Mark (B)
From French Marc, which itself comes from Latin, meaning 'warlike'. Despite being one of the names of the four apostles, Mark is a mainly 20th-century addition, although in a relatively short time it has established itself as a classic.

Marlene (B)
Created especially for Marlene Dietrich, it was in fact a contraction of her full name, Maria Magdalene.

Marmaduke (B)
From Gaelic, meaning 'servant of Maedoc', but a name long associated with Yorkshire and particularly the area around Thursk where it appears in the 1379 Poll Tax list.

Marshal (B)
From the Old French, meaning farrier, this surname became a Christian name first in the United States and has now become accepted elsewhere.

Marta (G)
German form of Martha.

Martha (G)
Aramaic, meaning 'lady'. In the New Testament Martha was the sister of Mary Magdalen. The French version of the name is Marthe.

Martin (B)
French, derived from the Latin for 'warlike', but more correctly associated with the gentle St Martin of Tours whose feast day of 11 November is also celebrated as Armistice Day. A favourite French name it has also become an English classic since the 20s.

Martina (G)
Slavic feminine form of Martin, meaning 'warlike'. A Hungarian fourth-century soldier saint, five popes were named after him. The French form of the name is Martine.

Martyn (B)
Welsh form of Martin which has been interchangeable with the English form, Martin, since the late 19th century.

Marvin (B)
English form of the Welsh Mervin, meaning 'friend'.

Mary (G)
English form of the Hebrew Miriam, meaning 'wished-for'. Miriam passed into Greek as Mariam, and into Latin as Maria. In Scotland, the daughter of the 12th-century Malcolm III and Queen Margarete was christened Marie, or Mary. By the 18th century, one in five girls was christened Mary. At its height of popularity in the Victorian era, it has since suffered something of a decline.

Mary Anne (G)

Coined in the 18th century when there was a fashion for putting girls' names together in pretty combinations.

Mathilda (G)

Latin form of Old German 'mahtihildi', meaning 'strong woman of battle', and a favourite name of the royal house of Normandy. William the Conqueror's wife was called Mathilda. The name was revived in the mid-18th century when there was a fashion for names with the pretty 'a' ending. An alternative spelling is Matilda.

Matthew (B)

From Hebrew, meaning 'gift of the Lord'. St Matthew the Apostle was the writer of the first gospel. It was a popular name in the Middle Ages for its religious associations and has stayed in more or less steady use since, even enjoying a boom in the last 40 years.

Maude (G)

From Mahaud, the Old French form of Mathilda, meaning 'strong woman of battle'. It is a quintessential medieval name. With Joan, Elizabeth, Agnes and Alice, Maude made up the five most popular girls' names of the Middle Ages. Tennyson was responsible for its revival in the 19th century with his poem 'Maud' (1855). The Scots form is Maudie.

Maureen (G)

English form of the Irish Mairin which became popular in the present century for its romantic Irish flavour.

Maurice (B)

From Latin, meaning 'of the land of Morocco'. There was a third-century Moroccan, or Mauretanian, saint who was martyred in Switzerland and gave his name to St Moritz. The Old French form was Meurisse which later became Maurice. The name was adopted in England in the present century for its French feel.

Mavis (G)

From Old English, meaning 'song-thrush'.

Max (B)

Short form of Maximilian, Maxim and Maxwell which has become a name in its own right in the present century.

The young Royals

The birth of a baby to Lady Helen Windsor and Timothy Taylor on 6 August 1994 raised eyebrows when it was announced he was to be christened Columbus George Donald Taylor, the first baby in royal history to be given a name which is neither royal nor entirely recognizable as a Christian name. But while the winds of change blow around the christening fonts of the young British royals, Monaco's royal family maintains traditional names. Princess Caroline's children were baptized Andrea (b. 1984), Charlotte (b. 1986) and Pierre (b. 1987). Princess Stephanie and Daniel Ducruet chose the name of the royal house of France, Louis (b. 1992) and Pauline Grace for their daughter born in 1994.

Children of the Prince and Princess of Wales
William Arthur Philip Louis (b. 1982)
Henry Charles Albert David (b. 1984)

Children of Princess Anne and Captain Mark Phillips
Peter Mark Andrew (b. 1977)
Zara Anne Elizabeth (b. 1981)

Children of the Duke and Duchess of York
Beatrice Elizabeth Mary (b. 1988)
Eugenie Victoria Helena (b. 1990)

Children of the Duke and Duchess of Gloucester
Alexander Patrick Gregers Richard (b. 1974)
Davina Elizabeth Alice Benedikte (b. 1977)
Rose Victoria Birgitte Louise (b. 1980)

Children of the Duke and Duchess of Kent
George Philip Nicholas (b. 1962)
Helen Marina Lucy (b. 1964)
Nicholas Charles Edward Jonathan (b. 1970)

Maximilian (B)
From Latin 'maximus', meaning 'the greatest'. It was a Roman title of honour and was revived by the Hapsburg emperors in the 16th century and subsequently becoming a princely and aristocratic German name. It came into use in England in the 19th century, with the charming diminutive Maxim.

Maxine (G)
French feminine form of Maximilian, meaning 'the greatest', which has become popular since the 50s.

May (G)
Affectionate form of Mary which was first given to Princess Mary of Teck, who married George V, and was known within the royal family as May.

Meg (G)
Affectionate form of Margaret which dates from the Middle Ages.

Megan (G)
Welsh, an affectionate form of Margaret, meaning 'little child of light'. It came into English usage at the beginning of the 20th-century when there was a fashion for pretty Welsh names.

Mehetabel (G)
Aramaic, meaning 'God benefits'.

Melanie (G)
From Greek, meaning 'dark-complexioned'. In classical mythology, it also has the association of winter, this being the name given to the goddess of the crops who went into mourning in the cooler months. The name was revived for its classical feel at the end of the 19th century and has become a 20th-century favourite.

Melesina (G)
Frankish, meaning 'hard-working' and the name of the daughter of Charlemagne. It was sometimes used as a Christian name in the 18th century.

Meleina (G)
Greek, meaning 'honeyed', and the family name given to Anna Amalia Mercouri, or Melina Mercouri as a child. A variation is Melinda, meaning 'sweet-soft'.

Melissa (G)
Greek, meaning 'a bee'. In Greek legend, Melissa was the name of a beautiful nymph and her name is still used in Greece. It came into use in England first as a poetic and literary name in the 16th century and then fell into disuse before being revived at the end of the 19th century when there was a fashion for classical Greek names.

Melitta (G)
From Greek, the name of the balm plant.

Melody (G)
Puritan name found in the West Country.

Melusina (G)
English form of the French Mélusine. In French fairy tales, Mélusine is a water-sprite or mermaid.

Menna (G)
Welsh form of Mona.

Meraud (G)
Old Cornish, meaning 'little one of the sea'.

Mercedes (G)
Spanish, meaning 'mercies'. Maria de las Mercedes is one of the names for the Virgin Mary.

Meredith (B)
English form of the Welsh Meredydd, meaning 'greatness'. It came into use at the start of the present century when there was a great interest in Welsh names. Since the 60s it has also been used for girls.

Meriel (G)
From Ancient Celtic 'myr', meaning 'the sea' and a pretty alternative to Muriel. It seems to have come from Brittany at the time of the Conquest and was well-known and used interchangeably with Muriel throughout the Middle Ages.

Merle (G)
Old French, meaning 'blackbird'. It was popularized by the film actress Merle Oberon in the 30s.

Merlin (B)
English form of the Old Welsh Myrddin, meaning 'sea fort'.

Merrilyn (G)
Welsh form of Marilyn.

Mervin (B)
From Anglo-Saxon 'maerwine', meaning 'famous friend', a name found in Yorkshire and the Border Country from the Middle Ages onwards. It is also spelt Mervyn.

Meryl (G)
Welsh form of Meriel, meaning 'the sea'.

Meta (G)
Short form of Margaret which has been popular in Ireland since the 19th century.

Mhairi (G)
Gaelic form of Mary currently undergoing a renaissance in Scotland.

Mia (G)
Italian, meaning 'mine'.

Michael (B)
From Hebrew, meaning 'who is like God' and the name of one of the three Archangels, the others being Raphael and Gabriel, who led the heavenly hosts in the Book of Revelations. A favourite of the Eastern Orthodox Church

The psychology of names

Freud was aware of the importance of names and noted how strongly our like or dislike of particular names was linked to associations. The psychoanalyst J C Flugel argued that people actually fall in love because of the associations of names. The poet Byron was 'utterly devotedly fond' of Mary Duff when he was eight and had a weakness for Marys and Marions all his life.

But the most revealing body of work has been done recently into the way other people's reactions to our names affect our sense of self. In 1973 researchers in California asked teachers to assess eight school essays. Four of these essays were headed Michael, David, Karen and Lisa and four Elmer, Hubert, Bertha and Adelle. Although identical in standard, Michael and David outscored Elmer and Hubert by a full grade, suggesting an intolerance of unusual boys' names, while Karen and Lisa outscored Bertha and Adelle, but by a smaller margin.

Meanwhile a study at Sussex University in 1990 looked at how names are perceived in terms of their masculine and feminine qualities.

Top ten most masculine names
John, David, Richard, Peter, Mark, James, Paul, Michael, Matthew and Edward

Most feminine girls' names
Sophie, Elizabeth, Emily, Lucy, Rose, Emma, Katherine, Mary, Diana and Victoria

While there is some truth in these findings, they must also be taken with a pinch of salt. Teachers undoubtedly help to shape children's self-esteem, but while their like or dislike of a child may be affected by the child's name, it is just as likely to be affected by physical appearance, behaviour or the inner reaction that all of us have to other people. Equally, names which are perceived as being particularly masculine or feminine now may be quite different from those of ten years hence. Fashions in names change and perceptions with them.

The best advice to parents on the naming of children is to use common sense:

1. Give your child a name which is easy to pronounce and easy to spell. Although unusual names that are hard to pronounce will not *cause* shyness in a child they can make a shy child more sensitive.

2. Names can be movable feasts and children benefit from being known by different names in different contexts. A little boy named William may be called Willy by his parents, William by his grandparents, 'iliam by his brother, and Billy by his friends at school. At some point he will decide what suits him best.

3. There is scarcely a name in English usage which the vivid imagination of a group of seven-year-olds in the playground cannot turn into an unpleasant nickname, but parents of newborn babies often spend hours and hours fretting about the possible permutations of the names they like. Don't. All names are potential hostages to fortune, just choose one that you like.

it was the name of nine emperors of Constantinople and five kings of Romania but did not come into use in England until the 12th century. Written Michael but pronounced in the French way Michel, it is often used interchangeably with Miles. A great favourite of the 20th century.

Michaela (G)
Feminine form of Michael, meaning 'who is like God'. It is the name of Don José's loyal and gentle friend in Bizet's *Carmen*.

Michel (B)
French form of Michael which has come into English usage in the present century.

Michele (G)
French feminine form of Michel, or Michael which came into use in England in the 50s. It is also spelt Michelle.

Mildred (G)
From Anglo-Saxon, meaning 'gentle power' and the name of one of the early royal English saints. Her name was revived in the 19th century for its religious and historical associations.

Miles (B)
From Frankish 'milo', meaning 'merciful'. It was brought to England at the time of the Conquest and was immensely popular in the Middle Ages, often used as an affectionate form of Michael. Although it seems to have died out by the 17th century it has been revived in present times for its Old English feel.

Millicent (G)
English form of Frankish Melesina, meaning 'hard-working'. It was popularized in the 20s by Joyce Lankaster Brisley's book *Milly Molly Mandy*, the proper name of her heroine being Millicent Margaret Amanda.

Mimi (G)
French pet form of Marie. The German equivalent is Mitzi.

Minette (G)
Pretty French pet form of Henrietta, meaning 'little one who rules'.

Mirabel (G)
From Latin, 'mirabilis', meaning 'wonderful'. As Mirabella it was popular in the 18th century.

Miranda (G)
From Latin, meaning 'to be admired', and the name of Shakespeare's heroine in *The Tempest*. It was a well-loved Elizabethan and Stuart name and has happily been revived in the present century.

Miriam (G)
Hebrew, meaning 'longed-for child', and the original form of Mary. In the Old Testament, Miriam was the sister of Moses and Aaron and it was a favourite Hebrew name. It was translated into Greek as Mariam. The Puritans revived Miriam and it has been in fairly regular use since.

Modesty (G)
Puritan virtue name which has fallen into disuse. Ironically it is now best known as the name of a ritzy strip cartoon, called *Modesty Blaize*.

Moira (G)
Scottish Gaelic Moire, and the name used for the Virgin Mary which was for a long time considered too sacred for use. In the 30s, 40s and 50s it was a popular Scottish name, although somewhat in decline now.

Molly (G)
Affectionate form of Mary and Margaret which may have originated as a rhyme for the Walloon name Polly, meaning 'a young girl'.

Mona (G)
English form of Irish Muadhnait, meaning 'noble'. It was the name of an Irish saint and also the Manx name for the Isle of Man.

Monica (G)
Greek, meaning 'one alone'. St Monica was an early saint and mother of Augustine, who brought Christianity to England. Her name came into use in the 17th and 18th centuries and has flourished in the present century.

Monro (B)
From Irish Gaelic, meaning 'man from the river Roe' in Derry. It has long been associated with Lowlands Scotland, however, and also appears with the spelling Monroe.

Montague (B)
French Norman from 'mont aigu', literally 'pointed hill'. It was the name of one of the companions of William the Conqueror who was later given landed estates in Somerset. Used as a Christian name in the 19th century for its aristocratic associations, the short form is Monty.

Mora (G)
From Gaelic, meaning 'the sun'. The diminutive is Morag.

Morag (G)
From Gaelic, meaning 'bright'. It is the Highlands form of Sarah, in the way that Sorcha is the Irish version of the name. Long popular in Scotland, Morag has come into general use in the present century.

Morgan (B)
From Old Welsh 'morien', meaning 'sea-borne' and a favourite Welsh name for centuries.

Morna (G)
From Gaelic 'muirne', meaning 'beloved'.

Mortimer (B)
Norman French, 'de Mortemer', meaning 'from Mortemer' and the name of one of the companions of William the Conqueror who settled in England. Used as a Christian name in the 19th century when there was a fashion for aristocratic names.

Morwenna (G)
Cornish name with Welsh origins, with the association of 'the sea'. A possible source is the Welsh 'morwaneg', meaning 'wave of the sea'. St Morwenna was Welsh but lived in Cornwall and the name has been in use there for many centuries.

Mungo (B)
From Irish 'mongach' meaning 'hairy'. It is best known through the 18th-century Scottish explorer Mungo Park

who travelled the road from the coast to Timbuktoo in West Africa.

Munro (B)
Scottish form of the Irish 'Monro', meaning 'man from the river Roe' in Derry and a popular Lowlands name.

Muriel (G)
Ancient Celtic, from 'myr' meaning 'sea'. An Irish form which developed from it is Muirgheal, meaning 'sea siren'. In use for over 1,000 years, it had become obsolete by Chaucer's time but was revived in the 19th century.

Murray (B)
Scottish clan name which took its name from the Celtic name for sea, 'myr' or 'mor'. It was adopted as a Christian name in the 19th century for its Scottish and aristocratic associations.

Myfanwy (G)
Medieval Welsh, meaning 'my rare one', a poetic Welsh name which has been in use there for many centuries, and in England since the 19th century.

Myra (G)
Poetic name coined for literary purposes at the end of the 16th century.

Myrna (G)
Possibly from Old Irish 'muirne', meaning 'beloved'. Myrna Loy, the film actress, was apparently so called after a prairie railway station that stuck in her father's mind.

Myrtle (G)
English botanical name which came into use, like Erica and Bryony, at the end of the 19th century.

N

Nadia (G)
From Nadja, the Slavic form of the Russian Nadezhda, meaning 'hope' which came into use in England towards the end of the 19th century when there was a fashion for Russian names.

Nadine (G)
French form of the Russian Nadezhda, meaning 'hope'.

Nan (G)
Affectionate form of Anne and Nancy, with the meaning of 'little graceful one'. The French diminutive is Nanette.

Nancy (G)
Form of Anne that came into use in the 18th century, meaning 'little graceful one'. The Welsh form is Nansi.

Naomi (G)
Hebrew, meaning 'pleasant'. Naomi appears in the Old Testament Book of Ruth and was revived by the Puritans in the 17th century for its biblical associations. Rare in the 18th and 19th centuries it has become popular again in recent years.

Napoleon (B)
From Italian, meaning 'someone from Naples'. Although chiefly associated with Napoleon Buonaparte, it was also the name of a fourth-century saint, and therefore has a place in the Christian calendar. Rarely in use in England, it has been a popular Christian name in the Caribbean and Southern states of the United States.

Nat (B)
Short form of Nathaniel.

Natalia (G)
From Latin 'natale Domini', meaning 'the birthday of the Lord' or 'Christmas Day'. The name passed into Russian

Most popular names of the century

In 1994, CACI Information Services analysed the census data of 22 million homes. What they found was that names were an accurate guide to age and could also indicate marital status. Of Britain's 479,000 Susans, only 15% are single, whereas nearly a quarter of the 730,000 Margarets and one in six of the 450,000 Williams live alone. Andrews were likely to be between 20 and 34, Peters between 30 and 59, Kenneths between 60 and 69, Christines between 35 and 49, Patricias between 40 and 64, and so on. Only two names belonged to all age-groups: Elizabeth and James. But most astonishing of all, is that one in twenty-five men, 1,259,000 are called John.

In order of popularity the names of the century are:

Boys: John, David, Michael, William, Peter, James, Robert, Paul, Stephen, Andrew, Richard, Alan, George, Mark, Thomas, Christopher, Brian, Ian, Anthony and Kenneth.

Girls: Margaret, Mary, Susan, Elizabeth, Patricia, Jean, Joan, Christine, Kathleen, Janet, Dorothy, Linda, Barbara, Karen, Julie, Helen, Ann, Jane, Sarah and Catherine.

---

as Natalya, with the diminutive Natasha. St Natalya was a favourite saint of the Russian Orthodox Church and her name has been popular for nearly a millennium in Russia.

Natalie (G)
French form of Natalia, meaning 'born at Christmas'.

Natalina (G)
Italian affectionate form of Natalia.

Natasha (G)
Russian diminutive of Natalya, literally meaning 'little Natalya' but with the association of being born at Christmas. It is a relatively recent addition to English names, but has become very popular in the last 35 years.

Nathan (B)
Hebrew, meaning 'gift'. A name in its own right in the United States, it is also used as a short form of Nathaniel.

Nathaniel (B)
Hebrew, meaning 'gift of God'. It was in use in Shakespeare's day, and was a favourite with the Puritans for its biblical associations, but is a name most associated with the United States.

Neal (B)
From Irish Néill, meaning 'champion', an alternative spelling of Neil.

Ned (B)
Short form of Edward which dates from the 14th century.

Neil (B)
English form of the Irish Néill, meaning 'champion'. It came into use in the early years of the 20th century and has been a firm favourite.

Nelson (B)
Heroic surname of Admiral Horatio Nelson which has since been used as a Christian name. Its most famous contemporary bearer is Nelson Mandela.

Nerina (G)
Latin, meaning 'sea-nymph'.

Nerissa (G)
Latin, meaning 'sea-nymph'. Nerissa was a companion of Portia in Shakespeare's *The Merchant of Venice*.

Nerys (G)
Welsh, meaning 'noble'.

Nesta (G)
Welsh form of Agnes which has also been in English usage this century.

Nestor (B)

Greek, meaning 'remembrance'. In Greek mythology, Nestor was a wise old man.

Neva (G)

Spanish, meaning 'snow'.

Neville (B)

French Norman, literally 'from Neuville', a village near Dieppe. Gilbert de Nevil was a companion of William the Conqueror and the Nevilles became a powerful dynastic family in England's medieval history. Shakespeare refers in *Henry VI Part II* to 'The Nevilles all, whose swords have never been drawn in vain'. The name was popular in the 19th century when there was a fashion for aristocratic names.

Nial (B)

Scottish form of Irish Gaelic Niadh, meaning 'champion'. Robert the Bruce's younger brother was called Nial, pronounced in the Highlands way, 'Neal'. He was also known interchangeably as Nigel, from the Latin form of the name Nigelus.

Niall (B)

Modern Irish form of Irish Gaelic Niadh, meaning 'champion'. Niul 'of the nine hostages' was a fifth-century Irish king and his descendants, the O'Neills, ruled Ulster for many centuries. The Irish pronunciation is 'Neel', the English is 'Nye-al'.

Niamh (G)

Irish, meaning 'bright'. In Irish mythology she is a princess who takes the poet Ossian to the Land of Promise.

Nicholas (B)

From Greek Nikolaos, with the associations of victory and people. St Nikolaos of Myra was a popular early saint whose name spread to Russia and also to Western Europe. The name was used by monks before the Norman Conquest and appears in the Domesday Book. One of the great English names, it has been in more or less constant use for nearly 900 years.

Position in the family

Pedzi, meaning 'finisher', is the name given by the Mashona people of Zimbabwe to the last boy born into the family, Taro to the first-born son in Japan. In Nepal children are called affectionately by their position in the family ('Zetsa, or 'eldest son', 'Maili' or 'second daughter', 'Kaila' or 'fourth son' and so on) as well as by their given names.

Roman:
Quintus (fifth son), Sextus (sixth son), Prima (first daughter), Secunda (second daughter), Tertia (third daughter)

Cornish:
Kensa (first daughter), Nessa (second daughter), Tressa (third daughter), Peswera (fourth daughter)

Nepalese:
Zetsa (first son), Maila (second son), Saila (third son), Kaila (fourth son), Thaila (fifth son), Zetsi (first daughter), Maili (second daughter), Saili (third daughter), Kaili (fourth daughter), Thaili (fifth daughter)

Santee:
Winona (first daughter)

French:
Benjamin (last son of the family)

Nico (B)
Greek short form of Nicolas.

Nicolas (B)
Original English spelling of Nicolaus, the Latin form of the Greek Nikolaos. The 'h' of Nicholas crept in in the 12th century.

Nicola (G)
Italian feminine form of Nicolo, with the association of

victory and people. A medieval name of great charm, it appears often in European legends and romances. The Italian diminutive is Nicolina.

Nicole (G)
French feminine form of Nicholas which dates from the Middle Ages. The diminutive, which means 'little Nicole', is Nicolette.

Nigel (B)
From Latin nigellus, meaning 'black' but used from the sixth century as the scholastic form of the Celtic Irish Niall and eventually becoming a name in its own right. Its great popularity in the 19th century was due to Sir Walter Scott's adventure novel, *The Fortunes of Nigel*.

Nigella (G)
Feminine form of Nigel which may have originated in Scotland. It was quite often used at the end of the 19th century for its botanical associations.

Nils (B)
Scandinavian form of the ancient Celtic name Niadh, meaning 'champion', which passed into modern usage as Nial, Niall, Neal and Neil. The Icelandic form is Njal.

Nina (G)
Russian affectionate form of Anna. In Spanish it is the word for 'child'.

Ninian (B)
Celtic, the name of a fifth-century saint who converted part of Scotland to Christianity. His name was used for many centuries in Scotland and at the end of the 19th century was generally revived.

Noah (B)
From Hebrew, meaning 'long-lived'. It seems to have been a name which was known in different cultures of the Middle East and not just to the Israelis. There was, for example, a Sumerian called Noah Zi-ud-Sudda or 'life of days long'. It was revived by the Puritans for biblical associations.

Noel (B)
French, meaning 'Christmas'. It was traditionally given to

children born on Christmas Day and was very common in the Middle Ages and has benefited from something of a renaissance in the 20th century.

Noelle (G)
French feminine form of Noel given to girls born on Christmas Day.

Noor (G)
Royal Arabic name, meaning 'light'.

Nora (G)
Short form of Latin honora, meaning 'honour' which has become a name in its own right.

Norah (G)
Irish shortened form of Latin Honora, meaning 'honour'.

Noreen (G)
Irish diminutive of Nora. It also has the variations of Norinna and Norine. The true Irish is Noirin.

Norma (G)
From Latin, meaning 'rule'. Norma was made popular as a name by the heroine of Bellini's opera in which she is a Druidic princess secretly married to a Roman.

Norman (B)
Old English name, meaning 'man from the north'. It was a description of the Viking invaders, the Norse – or North – men. Although it died out in the Middle Ages in England, it was kept in use in Scotland. Revived in the 19th century it was a popular Edwardian name.

Nowell (B)
English form of the French Noel, meaning 'Christmas'. It was given to children of both sexes born at that time but is now thought of as a boy's name.

Nuala (G)
Irish pet name for Fionnghuala.

Nye (B)
Welsh pet form of Aneurin.

O

Oberon (B)
Shakespeare's version of the French Auberon, meaning 'elf-rule'. In French medieval romance he was the mischievous king of the fairies.

Octavia (G)
From Latin, the name of a powerful patrician family whose name literally means 'eighth child'. Octavia was Mark Antony's wife.

Odette (G)
French affectionate form of Odile which has been adopted into English in the last 40 years. Odile derives from Old German, St Odile or St Ottilie being the patron saint of Alsace.

Olaf (B)
From Old Norse, a royal Danish name with the associations of 'ancestor remains'. It was sometimes used in this country in the 19th century for its historical and Nordic feel.

Olave (B)
From Old Norse, meaning 'ancestor'. The modern Scandinavian form is Olaf.

Olga (G)
Ancient Russian, from 'helga', meaning 'holy' and one of the most popular girls' names in Russia for its association with the tenth-century St Olga. It came into use at the beginning of the present century when there was a fashion for Russian names.

Olive (G)
From Latin, meaning 'olive'. St Olivia was an early Roman martyr and her name appears as Oliff in records of the Middle Ages. It was superseded by the Italian form Olivia

in the 16th century, but reappears as Olive from time to time in the last and present century.

Oliver (B)
English form of the French Olivier, of unknown meaning. Olivier, however, was one of the knights or paladins of Charlemagne's court in the ninth century and his name appears often in medieval romances. The name was brought to England at the time of the Conquest and was quite common until the 17th century when, on account of Oliver Cromwell, it fell from favour. It was revived in the 19th century for its medieval feel.

Olivia (G)
Italian, meaning 'olive'. Shakespeare chose the name for his wealthy countess in *Twelfth Night*. Pretty girls' names which ended in 'a' were popular in the 18th century and in the present century, too, Olivia has been in steady use.

Olwen (G)
Welsh, meaning 'white footprint'. The story of Olwen and the Prince Culhwen is told in the ancient book of Welsh legend, the *Mabinogion*.

Olympia (G)
From Greek, meaning 'heavenly'. Olympia was the mother of Alexander the Great.

Oonagh (G)
Old Irish, from 'uan', meaning 'lamb'. The anglicized form is Oona.

Opal (G)
Jewel name coined at the end of the 19th century.

Ophelia (G)
From Greek, meaning 'help-mate'. It was coined by an Italian poet called Sannazaro in the 16th century and immortalized by Shakespeare in *Hamlet*.

Oriel (G)
From Old French, meaning 'window' and a pretty medieval name.

Old English names

What we call Old English names are Anglo-Saxon and date from the sixth century. The Anglo-Saxons were a group of Germanic tribes who invaded Britain when the Romans departed and by the eighth century they had divided the country into seven kingdoms, each of which had a royal house with their own stock of names. Unlike the poetic Celtic names, Anglo-Saxon names are curiously functional in their meanings. Edward, for example, comes from 'ead' meaning 'rich' and 'weard' meaning 'guardian', Edgar from 'ead' and 'gar' meaning 'spear'. Names were passed on from generation to generation by keeping one element the same and adding another. Names of the royal house of Northumbria all begin with 'Os' meaning 'a god', those of Kent with 'Aethel' meaning 'noble' and Wessex with 'Ead' or 'Aethel'.

Boys

Alfred 'elf counsel'
Edgar 'prosperous by the spear'
Edmund 'guardian of prosperity'
Edward 'guardian of prosperity'
Edwin 'friend of prosperity'
Edwy 'beloved of prosperity'
Osborn 'warrior of God'
Oscar 'spear of God'
Osmund 'divine protection'
Oswald 'power of God'
Osric 'rule of God'
Oswin 'rule of God'

Girls

Edith 'prosperous in war'
Edwina 'friend of prosperity'
Elgiva 'elf gift'
Emma 'whole'
Mildred 'mild power'

Orlando (B)
Italian form of Roland which was popular in the 16th century when there was a vogue for European names.

Orson (B)
From Latin, meaning 'little bear'. *Valentine and Orson* was a medieval romance which told the tale of two brothers. The name remains popular in France.

Osbert (B)
Old English, one of the names of the royal house of Northumbria, meaning 'bright as God'. It died out with the Norman Conquest, but was revived for its historical flavour at the end of the 19th century.

Oscar (B)
Old English, meaning 'spear of God'. Taken to Ireland by the Danes as Osgar in the eighth century. It was revived in the 18th century across Europe when a Scottish book dealer 'discovered' the poems of the third-century bard Ossian whose son was called Oscar. Napoleon loved the name and insisted that his godson, who later became king of Sweden, was called Oskar. By a similar root it was passed to the most famous Oscar of all: Oscar Wilde's father was physician to the second king Oscar of Sweden and the young Master Wilde, who was his godson, was so named in his honour.

Osmund (B)
Old English, meaning 'divine protection' and one of the names of the royal house of Northumbria.

Oswald (B)
Old English, one of the names of the royal house of Northumbria, meaning 'power of God'. Unlike Osbert and Osborn, it remained sporadically in use until the 18th century, before undergoing a popular revival for its historical flavour at the end of the 19th century.

Oswin (B)
From Old English, one of the names of the royal house of Northumbria, meaning 'rule of God'.

Otis (B)
From Greek, meaning 'keen-eared'.

Ottilie (G)

From Old German, meaning 'homeland'. St Ottilia was a seventh-century martyr who became patron saint of Alsace. It has remained a favourite Dutch name, pronounced Oh-til-lee.

Owain (B)

Welsh, meaning 'well-born', suggesting it was a noble or princely name. The name appears many times in ancient Welsh legend, but the most famous Owain of all was Owain Glyndyfrdwy, or Owen Glendower, the 15th-century uncrowned King of Wales.

Owen (B)

English form of the Welsh Owain, meaning 'well-born'. It became popular at the end of the 19th century when there was a great interest in old Welsh stories and legends.

P

Pablo (B)
Spanish form of Paul. The Italian form is Paolo.

Pádraic (B)
Modern Irish, meaning 'nobleman'. It is one of the great Irish Celtic names, rendered Patrick in English, and the name of St Pádraic or St Pádraig, the patron saint of Ireland.

Padrig (B)
Welsh form of Patrick.

Paloma (G)
Spanish, meaning 'dove'.

Pamela (G)
From Greek 'pan meli', meaning 'all honey', a name made up by the 16th-century poet Sir Philip Sidney and initially pronounced Pam-e-ela. It was immortalized by Richardson 160 years later in his novel *Pamela, or Virtue Rewarded* (1740) and has been more or less in continuous use since. A variation is Pamelia.

Pandora (G)
From Greek 'pan dora', meaning 'all gifts'. It came into use at the end of the 19th century when there was a fashion for classical names.

Pasco (B)
Cornish form of the French boy's name Pascal, from the Latin and Hebrew 'dies paschalis', literally day of Passover, or day of Easter, used for those born at these times.

Patience (G)
English virtue name which was brought into use in the 16th century by the Puritans. It has survived happily into the present century.

Patricia (G)

Latin, meaning 'noblewoman'. It came into use in the 18th century in Scotland, possibly as a feminine form of Patrick, and has long been popular there. In 1886 it was used as a Christian name for a granddaughter of Queen Victoria, who was christened Victoria Patricia but known as Patricia.

Patrick (B)

English form of the Irish Pádraic or Pádraic, meaning 'nobleman' and the name of Ireland's patron saint. His name was considered too sacred for use in Ireland until the 16th century, but in Scotland and the north of England it was in use from the Middle Ages. One of the classic names of the present century, it first came into use over 100 years ago when there was a revival of interest in Celtic names.

Paul (B)

From Latin 'paulus' meaning 'small' and the name taken by Saul of Tarsus after his conversion. It was hardly known in England until the 16th and 17th centuries when it was adopted by the Puritans, but its fortunes fluctuated until the present century when it has become something of a classic.

Paula (G)

From Latin, meaning 'small' and the name of a fourth-century saint, who was known as Paulina. Her name, in both forms, appears in records of the Middle Ages, but has only achieved real popularity in the present century. Sir Arthur Pinero's *The Second Mrs Tanqueray* (1893) made it a popular Edwardian Christian name.

Paulette (G)

French feminine form of Paul, popularized by the 30s' film actress Paulette Goddard.

Pauline (G)

French feminine form of Paul made famous across Europe in the early 19th century by the beautiful Pauline Borghese, sister of Napoleon. Robert Browning brought the name to an English audience with his poem 'Pauline' in 1833 and it was subsequently adopted as a Christian name.

Pavel (B)
Russian form of Paul.

Pearl (G)
English jewel name coined at the end of the 19th century.
The French spelling is Perle.

Pedro (B)
Spanish form of Peter.

Peggy (G)
Affectionate form of Margaret which dates from the 16th
century. In the first half of the present century it was often
used as a name in its own right.

Penelope (G)
From Greek, meaning 'bobbin'. Penelope was the loyal wife
of the wanderer, Odysseus. It became a popular literary
name in the 17th century and was revived at the end of
the 19th century when there was a fashion for classical
names.

Penrose (B)
Monmouthshire place name, which has also become a
Christian name.

Peony (G)
Turn-of-the-century flower name, literally 'peacock flower'.

Pepe (B)
One of the most popular Spanish boys' names, with a pet
form of José.

Perceval (B)
Perceval, who killed dragons and rescued maidens, was a
hero of medieval romantic tales and as Peredur he is a
legendary Welsh hero. The name was sometimes used in
aristocratic families in the late 19th century.

Percy (B)
Family name which became a Christian name in the
19th century. The Percys of Northumberland came from
Normandy with William the Conqueror, and the popularity
of the name owes much to the poet Percy Bysshe Shelley
who was distantly related.

Choosing a name

Traditions of naming children vary the world over. The Maori of New Zealand recite a long list of ancestral names until the child sneezes, thereby indicating that a blessing has been given on that particular name. The Inuit Eskimos give their children the name of someone who has recently died in the community as a way of preserving the spirits of their ancestors, although if the baby cries a great deal it is taken as an indication that the name is not suitable. The remedy is for the midwife to recite a list of possible names until one silences the child, and this then replaces the name first given. In Hawaii children are named after events or omens in the parents' dreams. North American Indians call their children after the first significant thing noticed by the mother after her baby is born, such as Tallulah (running water), or Minnehaha (laughing water).

Perdita (G)
Invented by Shakespeare for the heroine of *The Winter's Tale*. He took it from the Latin word for 'lost'.

Peregrine (B)
From Latin, meaning 'traveller' or 'pilgrim'.

Perry (B)
Pet form of Peregrine and Peter which is popular in the United States.

Persephone (G)
Greek, with the association of spring.

Peta (G)
A Greek feminine form of Petros, meaning 'rock'. It is a favourite in Australia.

Peter (B)
One of the great European names, from the Greek Petros, meaning 'rock'. It was the name given by Jesus to the

The flourish of a pen

Names made up by writers

Pamela By the poet Sir Philip Sidney for his poem 'Arcadia' (1590) from the Greek 'pan' meaning 'all' and 'meli' meaning honey

Imogen By William Shakespeare for the heroine of his play *Cymbeline*. It has been suggested that he actually called her Innogen, but his writing was misread by the printers as Imogen

Lorna By R D Blackmore for his novel *Lorna Doone* (1869) from the Old English 'lorn' meaning 'lost' or 'forsaken'

Vanessa By Jonathan Swift for his friend Esther Vanhomrigh, from the first three letters of her surname which he combined with Essa, a pet form of Esther

Wendy By Sir James Barrie, for Wendy Darling in *Peter Pan* (1904) inspired by the little daughter of a friend of his who referred to him first as her 'fwendy' and then as her 'fwendy-wendy'

Thelma By Marie Corelli, for the title of her novel *Thelma, A Norwegian Princess* (1887), from the Greek 'thelema', meaning 'will'

Evangeline By Longfellow, for the heroine of his narrative poem 'Evangeline' (1847)

Fiona By William Sharp, a Scottish writer who wrote romances based on Scottish and Irish tales in the 19th century, as a pen-name (Fiona Macleod), from the Gaelic 'fionn' meaning 'fair'

---

disciple, Simon, whom he described as the rock upon which he would build his Church. The Latin form, Petrus, appeared in the Domesday Book, but Piers was generally more common in the Middle Ages. Its resurgence as a 20th-century classic owes much to J M Barrie's *Peter Pan*, which was first performed in 1904.

Petra (G)
Greek feminine form of Petros, or Peter, meaning 'rock'.

Petronella (G)
An Italian medieval name derived from the Greek Petros, or Peter.

Petula (G)
Latin, meaning 'seeker'.

Philip (B)
From Greek, meaning 'lover of horses' and a royal name of the house of Macedonia. Philip of Macedonia was the father of Alexander the Great, and his name, like his son's, spread far and wide across Greece and Asia Minor in the fourth century BC. With biblical and royal associations it became a favourite kingly and papal name across Europe in the Middle Ages and Renaissance, only being dropped in England for its associations with Philip II of Spain, husband of Mary Tudor. It was finally revived in the late 19th century when there was a fashion for classical Greek and Roman names and has become a favourite of the 20th century. The French form is Philippe.

Philippa (G)
Feminine form of Philip which was popular in the Middle Ages. It was brought to England by Philippa of Hainault, who married Edward III. It was revived in the 18th century and the poet Browning was fond of it and its diminutive Pippa, writing a well-known poem 'Pippa Passes' (1841).

Philomena (G)
From Greek, meaning 'a nightingale'. It was sometimes used as a Christian name in the 19th century.

Phoebe (G)
Greek, meaning 'the shining one', and one of the names given to the goddess of the moon. Its classical associations

made it popular with 16th-century poets and Shakespeare chose it as the name for a shepherdess in *As You Like It*. It was revived at the end of the 19th century when classical names were in fashion.

Phyllida (G)
From Greek 'phyllis', meaning 'a green branch'. In Greek legend, her name is associated with a maiden who turned into an almond tree after dying of a broken heart. It was a favourite of English poets writing pastoral and romantic verse.

Phyllis (G)
Greek, meaning 'a green branch'. One of the pretty classical names revived at the end of the 19th century.

Pia (G)
Latin, meaning 'pious'.

Pierre (B)
French form of Peter, meaning 'rock' or 'stone'.

Piers (B)
From French Pierre, meaning 'rock' or 'stone' and the medieval form of Peter. It was introduced by the Normans at the time of the Conquest and within 100 years had established itself as a quintessential English name, even being immortalized in the great allegorical tale of peasant life, William Langland's 15th-century *Piers Plowman*. Out of fashion for many centuries, it has enjoyed a revival since the 60s and is tipped as one of the most popular boys' names of the 90s.

Pippa (G)
Short form of Philippa brought into usage by Robert Browning's poem 'Pippa Passes' in 1841.

Polly (G)
From Dutch Walloon, meaning 'a young girl'. It was a popular 18th-century name and was immortalized as the name of the heroine Polly Peachum in John Gay's effervescent tale of highwaymen and maids, *The Beggar's Opera*.

Poppea (G)
Roman, the name of Emperor Nero's amber-haired wife.

Poppy (G)

Flower name coined at the end of the 19th century which has survived well into present times.

Portia (G)

From Latin, meaning 'offering' and the name of Shakespeare's heroine of *The Merchant of Venice*.

Priscilla (G)

From Latin 'priscus', meaning 'ancient'. The name was first adopted by the Puritans in the 17th century for its New Testament associations and revived again at the end of the 19th century for its classical feel.

Prudence (G)

One of the abstract virtue names favoured by the Puritans which came into use in the late 16th century.

Prunella (G)

Italian, meaning 'little plum'.

Psyche (G)

Greek, meaning 'soul'.

Q

Queenie (G)

English form of the Italian Regina and French Raine, meaning 'queen'. Queenie was traditionally the nickname of girls christened Victoria during Queen Victoria's reign.

Quentin (B)

French form of the Latin 'quintus', meaning the 'fifth son'. From the end of the Middle Ages it was most popular in Scotland, which had long links with the French court. Sir Walter Scott's novel *Quentin Durward* (1823) brought the name into general use. The more authentic Latin spelling is Quintin.

Quincy (B)

Norman aristocratic surname deriving from the town of Cuinchy, north of Arras. It became a Christian name in the United States following the popularity of John Quincy Adams (1767–1848), sixth President of the United States.

R

Rabbie (B)
Scottish familiar form of Rob and Robbie which dates from 18th century.

Rachel (G)
From Hebrew, meaning 'ewe', which was considered a symbol of gentleness and innocence. It was a favourite Jewish name for centuries and in the 17th century was adopted by the Puritans for its biblical associations. It has been a popular name in this country particularly since the 60s and it now stands in the top ten of girls' names.

Raine (G)
French, from 'reine' meaning 'queen'. The Italian form is Regina.

Ralph (B)
From Old Norse, with the royal associations of 'counsel' and 'wolf'. Passing into Norman French as Radulf and brought to England, it was written Rauf or Ralf and pronounced Rafe. It was an aristocratic name and only came into general use in the present century, when the 'l' was pronounced for the first time.

Ramona (G)
Spanish feminine form of Raymond.

Ramsey (B)
Scandinavian, meaning 'Ram's island' and a name associated with Ramsay MacDonald.

Ranald (B)
Highland Scottish form of Ronald. The Gaelic form is Raonull.

Randal (B)
From Old English, with the associations of 'shield' and 'wolf', suggesting it was a warrior name.

Randolph (B)

English, coined in the 18th century in the Churchill family, from the English Randal and the Norman French Ranulf. It came into general use in the 19th century for its aristocratic feel.

Ranulf (B)

From Old Norse, with the associations of shield and wolf, suggesting it was a warrior name. It passed into Norman French as Ranulf and was introduced to England at the time of the Conquest. For many centuries it has been associated with the Fiennes family.

Raoul (B)

French and Spanish form of Ralph which has sometimes been used in England.

Ray (B)

Short form of Raymond, which has almost become a name in its own right, meaning 'counsel'.

Raymond (B)

French, from Old German, with the associations of counsel and protection. It was both a heroic and religious name, a favourite of medieval Counts of Toulouse and of the Crusaders. John Masefield (1878–1967) revived it for his children's story *The Box of Delights*, and brought it into general use.

Rebecca (G)

Hebrew, meaning 'heifer' and with association of faithful wife. In the Old Testament Rebecca was the wife of Isaac and mother of Jacob, and much noted for her beauty. The Puritans revived her name for its biblical associations, sometimes spelling it Rebekah, which was translation which appeared in the King James I Authorized version of the Bible. It has been an immensely popular name this century.

Regina (G)

Latin, meaning 'queen'.

Reginald (B)

Old English, meaning 'power'. It came into use in the 19th century as a result of Sir Walter Scott's *Ivanhoe* (1820) which featured and was quickly adopted for its aristocratic feel.

Renata (G)
Italian, meaning 're-born'. The French form is Renée.

Reuben (B)
Hebrew, meaning 'behold a son'. In the Old Testament Reuben was one of the sons of Jacob.

Rex (B)
Latin, meaning 'king'. It came into being as a nickname for boys christened Reginald after the accession of Edward VII in 1901. Rexes Harrison, Whistler and Warner were all born in the early 1900s.

Rhea (G)
Greek, the name of the ancient earth goddess.

Rhiannon (G)
Welsh, meaning 'nymph' or 'goddess', pronounced Ree-ann-on.

Rhoda (G)
Greek, meaning 'rose'. Rhodes is, literally, the island of roses. A Rhoda appears in the New Testament, opening the door to St Peter who had escaped from Herod's prison. An 18th-century variation is Rhodabel.

Rhodri (B)
Old Welsh, a royal Welsh name, meaning 'circle-ruler', the circle being a reference to a crown. Rhodri the Great was the eighth-century King of North Wales.

Rhona (G)
Short form of the Old English Rowena meaning 'fair and slender'.

Rhun (B)
Welsh, meaning 'grand'.

Rhys (B)
Old Welsh noble name, meaning 'rashness'. Rhys ap Thomas was a powerful Welsh lord of the 15th century, a thorn in the English king's side. It remains a favourite Welsh name.

Richard (B)
From Anglo-Saxon and Norman, with associations of rule and hardness. The popularity of the name was due to

Richard the Lion Heart and his crusades to the Holy Land. It was the name of three English kings of the Middle Ages and has stayed within the top six names for boys ever since.

Richenda (G)
From Old German, meaning 'ruler', a pretty feminine version of Richard which has been traditionally associated with Devon.

Rick (B)
Nickname for Richard which dates from the Middle Ages. Richard had lots of short forms, including Dick, Hick and Dickon. Ricky is modern.

Rita (G)
Short form of Margharita, the Italian form of Margaret. It was made popular by Margharita Hayworth, better known as Rita.

Rob (B)
Very old shortened form of Robert which appears in the Domesday Book. Rob Roy was a great Scottish hero.

Robert (B)
From Old German, with associations of 'fame' and 'bright' and brought to England by the Normans. It was a noble and kingly name which became particularly popular in Scotland. Variations include Robin, Rob, Robbie, Rab and Rabbie.

Roberta (G)
Feminine form of Robert, with the associations of 'fame' and 'bright'. It is common in the United States.

Robin (B)
French, meaning 'little Robert'. It was more popular in the 13th century than Robert, its most famous owner being Robin Hood. Robin was also the name given to the bird known as the Redbreast. It became a favourite name in the 20s through its association with A A Milne's character, Christopher Robin.

Robina (G)
Scottish feminine form of Robin.

Puritan names

It is to the Puritans that we owe some of the pretty virtue names of the 17th century. Constance, Patience, Prudence, Verity, Hope, Faith, Honor and Tacey all date from this period, along with the less attractive Obedience, Silence, Tribulation and Acceptance.

Following the Reformation of the Church of England in the 16th century, Old Testament names such as Joshua, David, Daniel, Deborah, Sarah, Judith and Rebecca had already been adopted into general use (Shakespeare called one of his daughters Judith and another Susannah), so the Puritans, wishing to set themselves apart from the 'godless masses' were forced to go to plough deeper into biblical texts. Elijah, Zachary, Ebenezer, Caleb, Micajah and Seth were brought into use, but also phrases taken from the Bible such as Fear-not, PraiseGod, Sorry-for-Sin, even Flie-fornication appear as names in parish registers of the 17th century, while among the passengers on the *Mayflower* (1620) were to be found a Love and Wrastle Brewster, Remember Allerton, Humility Cooper and Resolved White.

In fairness only four per cent of Puritan children were given such names, although the practice lingered on in America as late as 1766 a child was christened Preserved Fish in New England.

Roderick (B)

From Old German, with associations of fame and rule. Its swashbuckling feel came from Smollett's 18th-century novel which had Roderick Random as its eponymous, adventurous hero and Scott's poem 'The Vision of Dom Roderick' which celebrated the life of the last Gothic King of Spain.

Rodney (B)

Surname which became a Christian name at the end of the 18th century through the deeds of Admiral Lord George Rodney who captured seven French ships in a battle off Dominica. A popular name in the 20s.

Roger (B)

From Anglo-Saxon and Old German, with the associations of fame and spear. It was a favourite Norman aristocratic name but died out in the 16th century, to be revived at the end of the 19th.

Roland (B)

From Old German, with associations of fame and land. Roland was a knight at the court of Charlemagne and the *Chanson de Roland* is a classic of early French literature. The name was introduced by the Normans and was immediately popular, although by the 16th century the spelling had become Rowland.

Rolf (B)

Old German, with associations of fame and wolf. It was supplanted by Ralf, but has been revived in the present century.

Rolph (B)

Scottish version of Ralph.

Romaine (G)

French, meaning 'someone who comes from Rome'. A variation is Romana.

Romola (G)

Italian feminine form of Romulus. George Eliot used it for the heroine of her eponymous novel (1863).

Romy (G)

German short form of Romaine and Romana.

Ronald (B)

Old Norse, Rognvaldr, which passed into Scottish as Ronald or Ranald. The Gaelic form is Raonull.

Rory (B)

English form of the ancient Irish Gaelic Ruadrhi and Scottish Gaelic Ruaridh, both meaning 'red'. Ruadrhi was a royal name, the name of three high kings of Ireland.

Rosa (G)

Latin, meaning 'rose'. It is found in medieval records but was most popular in Victorian times when flower names came into fashion. The 16th-century St Rosa of Lima, who was the first South American saint, caused the name to become widespread in Spain and Italy.

Rosaleen (G)

Irish form of Rose.

Rosalie (G)

From Latin 'rosalia', meaning 'garlands'. St Rosalia is the patron saint of Palermo in Sicily.

Rosalind (G)

From Old German, and associated with two sacred creatures, the horse and the serpent. Roslindis, as it was, was brought to Spain by the Goths and passed into Spanish as Rosalinda. It is a name which for many centuries has carried the sweet associations of the rose. Shakespeare immortalized Rosalind in *As You Like It*.

Rosamund (G)

Originally from Old German Rosmunda but often with the Latin sense of rosamundi, or 'rose of the world'. The spelling Rosamond is French.

Rosanna (G)

Italian, meaning 'little rose'. An alternative form is Rosetta.

Rosanne (G)

English form of Italian Rosanna which came into use in the early 19th century.

Rose (G)

Originally from Old German, but long associated with the queen of flowers. It was revived at the end of the 19th century when there was a great fashion for flower names.

Rosemary (G)

Created in the 18th century for a young woman christened Mary Dacre. Her family home was Rose Castle in Cumbria and when she married she was known as Rose-Mary. In the late 19th century there was a fashion for flower and herbal names and Rosemary came widely into use. An alternative spelling is Rosemarie.

Ross (B)
Scottish place name and surname, meaning 'cape' or 'peninsula'. In recent years it has been in the top ten of Scottish Christian names for boys and is a popular name in Australia.

Rowan (B)
English form of Irish Ruadhan, meaning 'little red one', or 'one with red hair'.

Rowena (G)
From ancient Celtic, meaning 'fair and slender'. It was a royal name born by the daughters of an early English king called Hengist. Sir Walter Scott called the heroine of his 1819 classic *Ivanhoe* Rowena and brought her name into general usage.

Rowland (B)
From Old German, with associations of fame and land, suggesting it was a royal or noble name. It was introduced to England by the Normans with the spelling Roland. Rowland is the English version.

Roxanne (G)
Persian for 'dawn' and the name of a princess who married Alexander the Great. The novel by Daniel Defoe, *Roxana* (1724), brought the name to a reading public in the 18th century and Edmond Rostand's *Cyrano de Bergerac* (1897) made it popular in France.

Roy (B)
From Scottish Gaelic 'rhu' meaning 'red-haired'. Sir Walter Scott's novel *Rob Roy* (1817) brought the name into use, and in the 20th century, which favours short names, it has been very popular both in its own right and as a short form of Royston.

Royston (B)
Surname deriving from a place name in Yorkshire which has been used as a Christian name this century.

Ruby (G)
Jewel name that was immensely popular at the end of last century.

Names for girls born at daybreak

Aurore
French, meaning 'dawn' and popular in France since the 16th century

Lucy
From Latin, meaning 'light'

Roxanne
Persian, meaning 'dawn'

Sara
Hebrew, meaning 'bright as dawn'

Aruna
Sanskrit, meaning 'dawn'

Usha
Sanskrit, meaning 'dawn'

Gwawr
Welsh, meaning 'dawn'

Brigid
Irish Celtic goddess of light, daughter of the Sun-god

Girls born in the middle of the night are traditionally called Nisha in India and Leila in the Arab world.

Rudolf (B)
From German and popularized by Anthony Hope's best-selling novel, *The Prisoner of Zenda*, which tells of the romantic and perilous adventures of English gentleman Rudolf Rassendyll in Ruritania. An alternative spelling is Rudolph.

Rudyard (B)
Coined by the Kipling family for their son who was

conceived during a family holiday at Lake Rudyard in Staffordshire in 1865.

Rufina (G)
Latin for 'rosy' or 'reddish'.

Rufus (B)
From Latin, meaning 'red-haired'.

Rupert (B)
From Old German, with the associations of fame and bright. The nephew of Charles I was Prince Rupprecht of the Rhine and became something of an English hero for his battle deeds. In this century it is associated with the poet Rupert Brooke and a bear!

Russell (B)
From French 'rousse' meaning 'red-haired'. It was a surname that became a Christian name for its aristocratic association with the Russell family.

Ruth (G)
From Hebrew, meaning 'friend'. The Book of Ruth is one of the most famous of the Old Testament. It came into use in England after the Reformation, when biblical names were much in fashion.

Ruthie (G)
Pet form of Ruth which may reflect the original pronunciation of the name, which in earlier centuries was written Ruthe.

Ryan (B)
Irish surname with the association of 'little king'. It has been used as a Christian name, particularly in Scotland, since the 70s and is currently the second most popular boys' name in Great Britain.

S

Sabina (G)
Latin, meaning 'woman from Sabine', a district neighbouring Rome. There was a fourth-century St Sabina and the name was in use in the Middle Ages. Despite the Reformation it remained in rural use until the 18th century and has been revived to some extent in the 20th century. The French form is Sabine.

Sabre (G)
Legendary name of the granddaughter of Brute, first King of Britain. Her name was Latinized to Sabrina.

Sabrina (G)
Latin form of Sabre, the name of the granddaughter of Brute, the first legendary King of Britain. She drowned in the River Severn, and her association with the river was celebrated by Milton in his masque *Comus* (1634).

Sacha (B)
Russian affectionate form of Alexander.

Sacheverell (B)
Norman aristocratic surname, meaning 'kid's leap' which derives from the castle of Saute de Chevreuil in Normandy. It was adopted by the Sitwell family in honour of William Sacheverell (1638–91), one of the founders of the Whig party.

Sadie (G)
Affectionate form of Sarah popular with the early settlers in America. Sairey continued in use in England until the 19th century.

Saffron (G)
English flower name associated with the crocus, and latterly with the model Saffron Aldridge.

Saladin (B)
From Arabic, meaning 'goodness of the faith'. Saladin was the great Kurdish prince, famed for his chivalry who defeated the Crusaders in Palestine in the 12th century.

Sally (G)
Affectionate form of Sarah, with the association of 'princess' which certainly was in use in the 17th and 18th centuries and possibly dates from medieval times, since it follows the pattern of familiar names then, eg Hal from Harry and Moll from Mary. It was popular in the 50s and 60s.

Saloman (B)
Hebrew, meaning 'peaceful'.

Salome (G)
Aramaic, meaning 'peace of Zion'. Its fateful association with the dance of the seven veils and John the Baptist has clouded its second appearance in the Bible, this time in the New Testament; she was one of the women to go the tomb of Jesus on Easter morning. It was a name used by the Puritans for this second association.

Salvator (B)
English form of the Italian Salvatore, meaning 'saviour'.

Samantha (G)
Probably Aramaic, meaning 'listener'. It is found in use among New England families in the 18th century, but came to popular use only in modern times. Grace Kelly played Samantha Tracy Lord in the 1956 film *High Society* and the long-running American television series *Bewitched* did a great deal to cement it as a contemporary favourite.

Samson (B)
Hebrew, meaning 'son'.

Samuel (B)
Hebrew, meaning 'heard by God' and the name of one of the great prophets of the Old Testament. It was rare until the 17th century but subsequently became a great favourite. Out of fashion from the mid-19th century, it has been well revived in recent times, with the short form Sam, as biblical names have returned to favour.

Sancha (G)
Spanish, meaning 'holy'. The Provençal form is Sanchia and was brought to England in the 13th century on the marriage of Richard Earl of Cornwall to Sanchia, daughter of the Count of Provence in 1243.

Sandra (G)
Short form of the Italian Alessandra, which came into use in the United States in the 50s. Also short form of the Greek Cassandra. Sandy is the American familiar form.

Sandro (B)
Italian short form of Alessandro.

Sapphira (G)
Hebrew, the name of the wife of Ananiar who appears in Acts of the Apostles.

Sapphire (G)
English jewel name which like Jade and Amber looks set to become a name of the 90s.

Sara (G)
Greek form of the Hebrew Sarah, meaning 'princess'. It was a name which appears frequently in medieval records, sometimes with the pretty diminutive Sarita. It is correctly pronounced Sar-ra.

Sarah (G)
Hebrew, meaning 'princess' and the name of the wife of Abraham, although she had originally been named Sarai, meaning 'quarrelsome'. It came into use in England in Elizabethan times and was immensely popular in the 17th century, although the form Sara was more common in the 18th and 19th centuries. In the present century it has been hugely popular since the 50s.

Saranna (G)
Combination of Sara and Anna which was in fashion in the 18th century.

Saskia (G)
Dutch form of Sarah, with the association of 'princess'. Rembrandt's wife was called Saskia.

The Gothic revival

The Return of Martin Guerre and *Cyrano de Bergerac* were two successful French films of the 80s (both of which, incidentally, featured Gérard Depardieu) which helped to establish a new mood in France for the medieval past. It even found its way on to the Parisian catwalks in a season of pared-down Gothic dresses in dark, flowing velvets. Bookshops, too, have been selling out of copies of the classic medieval French texts as smart parents rediscover the epic *Chansons de Geste*, among which is the great poem of French literature, the 11th-century *Chanson de Roland*. The next step, inevitably, was the christening font. In the fashionable 16th arrondissement of Paris, prams from Galeries Lafayette are less likely to contain baby Pierres, Jeans, Maries and Moniques as petits Rolands, Orsons, Maudes and Clothildes.

Bon chic bon gens names in Paris:

Boys	Robert	Bertille
Abélard	Roland	Blanche
Arnaud	Thibaud	Clothilde
Chrétien	Thierry	Etienne
Conrad	Tristan	Geneviève
Guillaume		Gertrude
Guy		Isabault
Hubert	**Girls**	Isolde
Ludovic	Aude	Mathilde
Orson	Béatrix	Maude
Renaud	Berthe	Roxane

Saul (B)
Hebrew, meaning 'asked-for' and the name of one of the first kings of Israel.

Scarlett (G)
American surname (of English origin) popularized as a Southern belle name as a result of Margaret Mitchell's *Gone with the Wind* (1936).

Scott (B)
Surname, meaning 'a Scott' which was first used as a Christian name in the United States and Australia. Since the 70s it has been warmly embraced by Scottish parents and is now the fifth most popular boys' name.

Séamas (B)
Irish form of James which dates from the 17th century.

Sean (B)
Irish form of John which originated in the Anglo-Norman Jean. The English spelling is Shaun.

Sebastian (B)
Latin, meaning 'from Sebastia', a town in Asia Minor. St Sebastian was a Roman legionary who was martyred in the third century and his name has been popular since medieval times in Italy and France. A curious variation is Bastian which can be found in Cornwall from the 16th century.

Selena (G)
From Greek, meaning 'moon' and one of the names by which the goddess Artemis was known. It was popular, for its classical associations, with English poets.

Selina (G)
English form of French Céline, meaning 'heavenly', first noted in England in 1619.

Selma (G)
Scandinavian, a short form of Anselma, meaning 'divine protector'.

Selwyn (B)
Welsh from Old English, meaning 'friend of the house'. It became a popular Christian name in Wales in the 19th

century for its association with George Augustus Selwyn, Bishop of Lichfield.

Senga (G)
Scottish version of Agnes, coined by reversing the letters, which was sometimes used in the 19th century.

Seraphina (G)
Italian, from Hebrew, meaning 'the bright one'.

Serena (G)
Latin, meaning 'serene' or 'calm'. It was one of the names used by Edmund Spenser in *The Faerie Queene* (1590–6) to address Elizabeth I.

Serge (B)
French form of the Latin Sergius, meaning 'attendant'. St Sergius of Radonezh was a 14th-century hermit who founded Russian monasticism (the Russian name is Sergei) and the name passed into French usage in the 18th century when there was great traffic between the French and Russian courts.

Seth (B)
Hebrew, meaning 'compensation' and the name of one of the sons of Adam and Eve.

Shannon (G)
From Irish, meaning 'the old one', the Shannon being the longest river in Ireland. In recent years it has become a very popular name in Scotland.

Shari (G)
Arabic form of the Hebrew Sharon.

Sharon (G)
Biblical place name, like Beulah, which was adopted by the Puritans. In the Song of Solomon, the tale is told of a virtuous Shulamite maiden who remains faithful to her shepherd in spite of the king's advances, and for this reason she is described as the Rose of Sharon. It was popular among the early settlers of New England and continued in use in America after its decline in popularity in England, although in recent times it is enjoying something of a revival.

Shaun (B)
English phonetic rendering of the Irish Sean, or John, which has been a popular name since the 60s.

Sheena (G)
English form of the Irish Síne, or Jean. The Scottish form is Shona or Sheona.

Sheila (G)
English form of the Irish Síle, with the association of 'heavenly'. It was popular in the 20s and 30s for its Irish associations.

Shelagh (G)
Modern Irish form of the old Irish Síle, meaning 'heavenly'.

Shelley (G)
Surname which was first used as a boy's name in the United States. Since the 50s it has been popular for girls on both sides of the Atlantic. The actress Shelley Winters was actually christened Shirley.

Sheryl (G)
American familiar form of Shirley which originated in the Southern states.

Shirley (G)
Yorkshire place name, meaning 'shire meadow' which was first used as a boy's name in the early 19th century. Charlotte Brontë adopted it as the name for the heroine of her novel *Shirley* (1849) and by the end of the century it was in general use. In the present century it received a huge boost in popularity as a result of Shirley Temple.

Sîan (G)
Welsh form of Jane which has come into English usage in modern times.

Sibyl (G)
From Greek, meaning 'prophetess'. The sibyls were women who foretold the future which was revealed to them by the oracles of the gods. It was a medieval name but subsequently fell into disuse. Benjamin Disraeli revived it for the heroine of his novel *Sibyl* (1845) and its classical

Names which appear in the Domesday Book

In 1086, 20 years after the Norman Invasion, William the Conqueror ordered a written survey of land holdings in England, both those which belonged directly to him as king, and those which were held by his feudal vassals, to assess the tax that could be raised on them. The survey, or Domesday Book as it came to be known, provides a fascinating insight into the baptismal names of the time. There are residual pockets of old English names, such as Oscar, Oswald, Kendric, Edward and Dunstan, but the majority such as Walter, Oliver, Ralph, Robert and William are Norman names. Probably these names had been assumed for politic reasons by existing landlords, or reflected the settlement of William the Conqueror's Norman companions. Just half a dozen women are listed as landowners – an Ingrid, Elgiva, Edith, Helewise, Mathilda and Adeline.

Names which go back over 900 years:

Adam	Dunstan	Helewise	Nicholas
Adeline	Edgar	Henry	Nigel
Alan	Edith	Hugh	Norman
Albert	Edmond	Ingrid	Oliver
Alfred	Edward	Jocelyn	Oscar
Andrew	Edwin	Joseph	Owen
Archibald	Elgiva	Laurence	Peter
Arthur	Gerard	Malcolm	Quintin
Bertram	Gilbert	Marmaduke	Richard
Brian	Guy	Mathilda	Robert
Constantine	Harold	Matthew	Roger
David	Harvey	Maurice	Roland

associations made it popular at the end of the 19th century. An alternative spelling is Sybil.

Sibella (G)
Latin form of Greek sibyl, meaning 'prophetess' which was occasionally used as a literary or poetic name. Sybella, daughter of Henry I of England married Alexander I of Scotland in the 12th century.

Sidney (B)
English aristocratic surname which came into use as a Christian name in the late 17th century among the gentry.

Sidonie (G)
French, with the association of 'linen' and the name traditionally given to girls born on the Feast of the Winding Sheet. It was the name of the French writer, Sidonie Gabrielle Colette. The English form is Sidonie.

Sigmund (B)
Old German warrior name, with the associations of 'victory' and 'protection'.

Sigrid (G)
Old Norse, meaning 'victory-ride'.

Síle (G)
Irish form of Celia, with the association of 'heavenly'.

Silvana (G)
From Latin, meaning 'wood-dweller'.

Silvester (B)
From Latin, meaning 'wood-dweller' and the name of three popes, the first of whom, it is said, was baptized by Emperor Constantine. In general use during the Middle Ages, it was revived at the end of the 19th century for its classical associations.

Simon (B)
Greek form of Hebrew Simeon, meaning 'he who hears', it is a name which appears many times in the Bible although it is most famously associated with Simon Peter, one of the first Apostles to be called by Jesus. Simon and Simeon were both in common usage in the Middle Ages, but largely fell

A rose by any other name – Shakespeare's heroines

It is to Shakespeare that we owe the popularity of names such as Jessica, Miranda, Imogen, Olivia and Rosalind. Since he could have plumped for the Elizabethan names of the time, such as Jane, Margaret, Mary and Joan, it seems fair to assume that he had a soft spot for pretty feminine names and took pleasure in creating poetic new ones and matching them to his characters. Perdita, for example, was coined from the Latin for 'lost'; Marina, with the association of 'sea', was used for the daughter of the King of Tyre, one of the great sea ports of the Mediterranean; and Imogen seems to have been minted originally from Innogen, meaning 'innocence'.

Adriana
  (*The Comedy of Errors*) wife of the young merchant of Ephesus
Audrey
  (*As You Like It*) Touchstone's beloved
Beatrice
  (*Much Ado About Nothing*) Benedick's sparring partner
Bianca
  (*The Taming of the Shrew*) Katharina's beautiful sister; (*Othello*) Cassio's mistress
Celia
  (*As You Like It*) friend of Rosalind
Cordelia
  (*King Lear*) Lear's faithful daughter
Cressida
  (*Troilus and Cressida*) lover of Troilus
Desdemona
  (*Othello*) wife of Othello

Diana
  (*All's Well That Ends Well*) zestful widow of
  Florence
Emilia
  (*Othello*) Iago's wife
Gertrude
  (*Hamlet*) mother of Hamlet
Helena
  (*All's Well That Ends Well*) a gentlewoman (*A Midsummer Night's Dream*) a young Athenian lady
Hermione
  (*The Winter's Tale*) Queen of Leontes
Hermia
  (*A Midsummer Night's Dream*) one of the young
  Athenian lovers
Hero
  (*Much Ado About Nothing*) daughter of the
  governor of Sicily
Imogen
  (*Cymbeline*) Cymbeline's daughter
Iris
  (*The Tempest*) the rainbow goddess
Isabella
  (*Measure for Measure*) sister of the aristocrat
  Claudio
Jessica
  (*The Merchant of Venice*) Shylock's daughter
Julia
  (*The Two Gentlemen of Verona*) lady of Verona
Julietta
  (*Measure for Measure*) Claudio's lover
Katharina
  (*The Taming of the Shrew*) the tamed shrew
Lavinia
  (*Titus Andronicus*) Titus's daughter
Luce
  (*The Comedy of Errors*) servant

Lucetta
  (*The Two Gentlemen of Verona*) Julia's servant
Maria
  (*Twelfth Night*) Olivia's lady-in-waiting
Mariana
  (*Measure for Measure*) Angelo's fiancée
Marina
  (*Pericles*) daughter of Pericles, Prince of Tyre
Miranda
  (*The Tempest*) Prospero's daughter
Nerissa
  (*The Merchant of Venice*) Portia's maid
Olivia
  (*As You Like It*) Countess of Illyria
Ophelia
  (*Hamlet*) Hamlet's betrothed
Paulina
  (*The Winter's Tale*) noble-hearted wife of
  Antigonus
Perdita
  (*The Winter's Tale*) 'the prettiest low-born lass,
  that ever/Ran on the green sward'
Phebe
  (*As You Like It*) shepherdess
Portia
  (*The Merchant of Venice*) heiress of Belmont
Rosalind
  (*As You Like It*) daughter of the banished duke
Sylvia
  (*The Two Gentlemen of Verona*) lover of Valentine
Tamora
  (*Titus Andronicus*) Queen of the Goths
Ursula
  (*Much Ado About Nothing*) Hero's maidservant
Viola
  (*Twelfth Night*) Sebastian's sister

into disuse after the Reformation. Simon has happily been revived in the present century and has enjoyed great popularity since the 60s.

Simone (G)
French feminine form of Simon which has sometimes been used as a Christian name in England in the present century.

Sinéad (G)
Irish form of Jane which is pronounced Shin-aid.

Siobhán (G)
Irish form of Joan, pronounced Shev-awn and a long-standing Irish favourite. The name Joan or Jhone was introduced in the 12th century by the Anglo-Normans.

Solange (G)
French, from the Latin 'Solemnia', meaning 'solemnity'.

Solomon (B)
Hebrew, meaning 'man of peace'.

Sonia (G)
English form of the Russian Sonya and Scandinavian Sonja, meaning 'little wise one', which came into use in England in the 20s.

Sonya (G)
Russian pet form of Sophia, meaning 'little wise one'.

Sophia (G)
Greek, meaning 'wisdom' and the name of an early Byzantine martyr. Emperor Justinian dedicated his great cathedral in Constantinople to Hagia Sophia, or Divine Wisdom. A royal Byzantine name, it passed into the Russian, Danish and German royal families and arrived in England in the 18th century as a popular name of the Hanoverian court.

Sophie (G)
French form of Sophia, meaning 'wisdom'. The English spelling is Sophy.

Sorcha (G)
Irish, meaning 'bright' and pronounced Sir-i-ca.

Speranza (G)
Italian, meaning 'hope'.

Stacey (G)
Short form of Anastasia, meaning 'resurrection' which originated in the United States.

Stanley (B)
English family surname of the earls of Derby, used latterly as a Christian name for its aristocratic flavour in the 19th century. It was given a boost by the famous 'meeting' of Henry Morton Stanley and David Livingstone at Ujiji on Lake Tanganyika in 1871 and was popular with Victorian and Edwardian parents.

Steen (B)
Affectionate form of Stephen, dating from the 16th century; Scottish form is Steenie.

Stefan (G)
German and Scandinavian form of Stephen, meaning 'crown'.

Stella (G)
Latin, meaning 'star' and coined by the soldier and poet Sir Philip Sidney in the 16th century for Lady Penelope Devereux.

Stephanie (G)
French feminine form of Stephen, used in England since the 20s. It is currently undergoing a revival, especially in Germany and Spain (as Estefania).

Stephen (B)
From Greek 'stephanos', meaning 'crown' or 'wreath' and the name of the first Christian martyr. His name was assumed by four popes and five Hungarian kings and became widespread on the Continent. Common in England in the Middle Ages, it fell into disuse until the 50s, since when it has blossomed again.

Steven (G)
English spelling of Greek Stephen, which dates from the 14th century and was most common as a surname. From

the 50s, when the name leapt to popularity, it has been interchangeable with Stephen.

Stewart (B)
Scottish clan name, meaning 'chief of the royal household'. It was the name of the royal house of Scotland from 1371 when Marjorie, daughter of Robert the Bruce, married Walter Stewart; the French spelling Stuart was adopted by Mary Queen of Scots in the 16th century. Used as a Christian name in this century.

Stirling (B)
Scottish place name, meaning 'easterling' or 'from the Baltic' which is sometimes used as a Christian name.

St George (B)
English saint's name, pronounced Sin-george.

St John (B)
English saint's name, pronounced Sin-jun.

Storm (G)
English 'nature' name which first came into use in the 60s.

Stuart (B)
Royal Scottish dynastic name that came into use as a Christian name at the end of the 19th century. The House of Stewart was the royal house of Scotland from 1371, and in the 16th century Mary Queen of Scots adopted the French spelling Stuart.

Sukey (G)
Affectionate form of Susanna or Susan which dates from the 17th century.

Susan (G)
Short form of Susanna, itself from the Persian Shushan and Hebrew 'shushannah', meaning 'lily', which came into use in the late 16th century. It more or less replaced Susanna as the popular form. One of the great Christian names of the 20th century.

Susanna (G)
English form of the Persian Shushan and Hebrew 'shushannah' meaning 'lily'; it has been in constant use since the Middle Ages.

Susannah (G)
From Hebrew 'shushannah' meaning 'lily', which itself came from the Persian Shushan, the name of a city known as the City of Lilies which is referred to in the Old Testament books of Esther and David. Shakespeare called his younger daughter Susannah.

Suzanne (G)
French form of Susanna, meaning 'lily'. The diminutive is Suzette.

Sylvia (G)
From Latin, meaning 'wood-dweller'. As Silvia it was a popular name during the Renaissance, and Shakespeare chose it as the name of one of his heroines in *The Two Gentlemen of Verona*. It was revived as Sylvia in the 19th century and was popular in the 30s and 40s.

Sylvie (G)
French form of Sylvia.

T

Tabitha (G)
Aramaic, meaning 'gazelle'. A Tabitha appears in the New Testament and for this reason it was adopted by the Puritans. Its pretty sound and meaning have made it a favourite in this century.

Tacey (G)
From Latin, 'tace' meaning 'be silent' and adopted by the Puritans in the 17th century as a virtue name.

Talbot (B)
Norman French, meaning 'wood cutter'. Richard de Talbot was a companion of William the Conqueror.

Tallulah (G)
American Indian, meaning 'running water'. It was popularized by the film star Tallulah Bankhead in the 20s.

Tam (B)
Scottish short form of Thomas, dating back to the 17th century.

Tamar (G)
Hebrew royal name, meaning 'date palm', and the name of the daughter and granddaughter of David.

Tamara (G)
Russian feminine form of the Hebrew Tamar, meaning 'palm tree'. Popular for its Russian feel in the last century.

Tamsin (G)
Cornish form of the English Thomasina and a feminine form of Thomas. It has become widely used outside Cornwall in the present century. An alternative spelling is Tamasin.

Australian names

Australian parents differ little from British ones in their choice of first names. The most popular names which appeared in the birth columns of *The Melbourne Age* for 1993 were:

Boys

Matthew	468	times
James	385	"
Daniel	292	"
Joshua	287	"
Michael	277	"
Benjamin	255	"
Luke/Lucas	253	"
Thomas	249	"
Nicholas	242	"
Jack	231	"

Girls

Jessica/Jessie	319	times
Emily	304	"
Sarah	259	"
Stephanie	236	"
Ashleigh/Ashley	231	"
Rebecca/Rebekah	182	"
Caitlin	180	"
Rachel	178	"
Emma	171	"
Lauren	170	"

Just as in Britain, old-fashioned names such as Edward, Charles, Andrew, Louise, Margaret, Mary and Grace live on as second and third names. And there are also similiar 'climbers' which look set to reach the top ten as the 90s progress: Callum, Jordan and Blake for boys, Chloë and the American Courtney for girls. A few names, however, are distinctive to Australia. Lachlan, an Australian boy's name of great pedigree,

Harrison, Mitchell and Angus all appear in the top fifty names and are unique to Australia. Annabel, Amelia and Elise are rare in Britain and the United States but are in steady use in the Antipodes.

Noticeably absent from the lists are Bruce and Sheila. Gone too are names such as Craig, Shane, Trent, Daryl, Brett, Clancy, Wayne and Norm for boys, Kylie, Nolene, Robyn, Sharleen, Narelle, Lindy-Ann and Raelene for girls. Doubtless they will return again in the next century when the patina of age makes them quaintly old-fashioned.

Tancred (B)
Old German, into French, with the associations of 'think' and 'counsel'.

Tania (G)
Pet form of the Russian Tatiana, also spelt Tanya. Russian names became popular in England at the turn of the century and Tania, like Natasha, Olga and Nadia has taken root and flourished.

Tansy (G)
Pet form of Anastasia.

Tara (G)
Irish, meaning the 'hill of Tara', Ireland's sacred mountain in County Meath where the High Kings of Ireland were crowned. It came into use as a Christian name at the end of the 19th century.

Tatiana (G)
Russian, possibly of Asiatic or Persian origin. St Tatiana was a third-century saint whose name is venerated in the Eastern Orthodox Church. An aristocratic and imperial Russian name.

Teague (B)
From Irish 'Teige' or 'Tadhgh', meaning 'poet'.

Ted (B)
Short form of Edward which, like Ned, dates from the 14th century.

Tegan (G)
Welsh, meaning 'beautiful and blessed'.

Terence (B)
From Latin, the family name of an important Roman clan, the Terentii. One of the best known bearers of the name was the Roman poet Terence, thought to have been an African and a slave by birth, but freed by his master for his good looks and intelligence. A fashion for classical names at the end of the 19th century brought his name back into use.

Teresa (G)
Spanish form of the Greek name Therasia, meaning 'to reap'. It became popular throughout Europe following the death of St Teresa of Avila in 1582.

Tessa (G)
English variation of Teresa, meaning 'one who reaps' which probably dates from the 19th century.

Thaddeus (B)
Hebrew, meaning 'valiant'.

Thea (G)
Short form of the Greek names Theodora and Dorothea, meaning 'of God'.

Thecla (G)
From Greek, meaning 'God-famed'.

Thelma (G)
An invention of the 19th-century novelist, Marie Corelli, who wrote a bestselling novel, *Thelma, A Norwegian Princess*. Corelli took the name from Greek 'thelema', meaning 'will'.

Theo (B)
Short form of Greek Theodore still in use in modern Greece.

Theobald (B)
An Old German name, meaning 'bold people' which passed into Italian as Tebaldo and Norman French as Theobald. Theobald evolved into the modern French Tibald.

Theodora (G)
Feminine form of Theodore, meaning 'gift of God'. It came into use at the end of the 19th century when there was a fashion for classical names.

Theodore (B)
From Greek Theodoros, meaning 'gift of God', the name of 27 Byzantine saints and a classic name which has passed happily into modern Greek. It was popular in the 19th century in the United States where it found a hero in Theodore Roosevelt. His pet name was Teddy and the teddy bear was named after him.

Theresa (G)
From French Thérèse which itself derived from the Spanish Teresa. Queen Marie Theresa of Austria popularized the name across Europe in the 17th century.

Thomas (B)
A biblical Aramaic name, meaning 'twin' and bestowed on one of the Apostles. It appears in the Domesday Book and was introduced by the Normans but quickly became an established English name. It has never been out of fashion and is now in the the top ten of boys' names in the country.

Thomasina (G)
A feminine form of Thomas which appeared in the Middle Ages. Its pet form Tamsin survived longer than the original name and has been popular in this century.

Thora (G)
Thor was the Old Norse god of thunder and Thora was introduced at the time of the Viking invasions. Associated with the north of England, it came into general usage at the turn of the century when there was a fashion for names from the distant past.

Thurston (B)
Old Norse, meaning 'Thor's stone' which like Thora stayed in use in Lancashire from the Middle Ages.

Tiffany (G)
From the Latin 'Theophania', meaning the season of the Epiphany and given to girls born at that time. It is a name associated with Cornwall.

Tilda (G)
A pet form of Matilda which became popular in the 19th century.

Timothy (B)
From the Greek 'timotheos', meaning 'God-fearing', it is famous through its biblical associations. Timotheus was a musician of Alexander the Great three centuries before Christ. It was brought into usage by the Puritans in the 17th century as a name which appeared in the New Testament but its popularity in this century is probably because of Beatrix Potter's Timmy Tiptoes.

Tina (G)
20th-century name which has been derived from Christina.

Titania (G)
Shakespeare used this name for the Queen of the Fairies in *A Midsummer Night's Dream*.

Titus (B)
Titus was a disciple of St Paul. His name was used by the Puritans in the 17th century but is rare today.

Tobias (B)
Hebrew 'Tobiah' and Greek 'Tobias', meaning 'God is good'. It was popular in the 16th century and was often given in literature in the form Toby to racy *bon viveurs*.

Toby (B)
Short form of Tobias which was popular from the 16th century. Its English feel and biblical associations tip it for a revival in the 90s.

Tony (B)
A short form of Antony and Anthony which was first recorded in the 17th century. By the 18th century it had a

'hail fellow well met' association, which it maintains nicely to this day.

Topaz (G)
One of the jewel names introduced at the end of the last century which has, perhaps unlike Pearl or Ruby, a more modern feel and is becoming more popular.

Torquil (B)
Anglicized form of Gaelic Torcail, meaning 'Thor's cauldron', Thor being the Norse god of thunder, and the name originally having been introduced by the invading Danes of the eighth century. As well as a favourite of the Macleod family, it has also been found in Yorkshire in the Middle Ages.

Tracy (G)
Norman aristocratic surname which has become a popular girl's name only in the present century. It is also spelt Tracey. The surge in popularity dates from the 50s when Grace Kelly played Samantha Tracy Lord in the film *High Society*.

Trefor (B)
Welsh 'tref', meaning 'homestead' and 'mawr', meaning 'great'. Tudor Trefor ap Ynyr was a tenth-century Welsh chieftain.

Trelawny (B)
Cornish place name. Sir Arthur Pinero's *Trelawny of the Wells* (1898) brought the name into use.

Tresilla (G)
Cornish place name, Tressillian. Trevena is another.

Trevor (B)
English form of the Welsh Trefor which came into use at the end of the 19th century when there was great interest in Welsh names and literature. It has been one of the most popular names of the century.

Tristan (B)
From medieval French, meaning 'tumult'. The tale of *Tristan and Iseult* was told by all the troubadours in France in the early Middle Ages.

The Battle for Bergamote

A desire by the state to preserve the purity of the French language, the decrees of the Council of Trent (1563) and the Revolutionary Law of II Germinal (1803) have all combined to keep French parents within strict bounds when naming their children.

The Council of Trent demanded that Roman Catholic priests baptize children only with the names of Catholic saints or New Testament Apostles, a measure designed to stamp out the spread of Old Testament names associated with the heretical Protestantism which was sweeping Northern Europe. In 1803 'persons known from ancient history', such as Alexandre, Ulysse, Honore, Jules, Marcel, Julie, Emilie and Sabine, were also permitted. And with this, free-spiritedness in the naming of children more or less came to an abrupt halt. In 1975 a Parisian architect wishing to name his daughter Bergamote was obliged to take his case to the High Court after being told by the public prosecutor's office that Bergamote 'was not a first name'. Arguing that Giscard d'Estaing had called his daughter Hyacinthe (supposedly after a flower although, in fact, it was also a saint's name) and that Myrtilles (the equivalent of our bilberry) were to be found aplenty, a barrister pressed the case that Bergamote (after a fruit) was not so farfetched. In surprisingly lenient mood the judge agreed, on the condition that a conventional saint's name accompany it. Bergamote Céline, the first in French history, was finally settled on.

On 8 January 1993, after more than 400 years, and amid much humming and haaing and column inches in *Le Monde*, all restrictions on names were lifted. The result? One in 20 boys in 1993 were named Kevin.

Tristram (B)
English form of Tristan. It derives from the ancient Celtic 'Drystan', meaning 'tumult' or 'din' and the name appears, like the legend of *Tristan and Iseult*, in Welsh, Cornish and Breton. By the 12th century, it had settled down into the form Tristram. The most famous Tristram of all is Laurence Sterne's young adventurer *Tristram Shandy* (1759), known for short as Trim.

Trixie (G)
Affectionate form of Beatrix and Beatrice sometimes used as a name in its own right.

Tudor (B)
Early Welsh form of the Greek Theodore, meaning 'God's gift'. A St Tudyr is found in Wales in the seventh century.

Tyrone (B)
Irish, meaning 'Owen's land' and the name of a county of Ireland. It came into use as a Christian name among Irish immigrants in the United States in the 19th century.

U

___

Ulla (G)

From Old Norse, related to Ulrika or Ulrica, and popularized by Sir Walter Scott in his novel *The Pirate* (1821) which is set in the Shetland Islands. Ulla is one of three daughters of Magnus Troil.

Ulrica (G)

Also spelt Ulrika, a modern Scandinavian name, derived from Old Norse, with the meaning of 'wolf ruler', suggesting that it was an ancient noble name.

Ulysses (B)

A heroic name, derived from the Etruscan 'Uluxe', the name for the Greek wanderer Odysseus, which was a popular name in the 19th century. Ulysses S Grant was 18th President of the United States.

Una (G)

English version of the Irish Oonagh or Oona.

Unity (G)

One of the virtue names created by the Puritans in the 17th century.

Unna (G)

Icelandic name, meaning 'woman'.

Ursula (G)

With the delightful meaning of 'little she-bear', Ursula has long been associated with this country, and particularly with Cornwall. Legend has it that a fifth-century Cornish princess called Ursula founded the order of Ursuline nuns. Shakespeare chose it as the name of his maid in *Much Ado About Nothing*.

Uwen (B)

English version of the Welsh Owen or Owain to be found in the Anglo-Saxon Chronicle.

V

Valentina (G)
Italian and Russian feminine form of Valentine, meaning 'strong' or 'healthy' and traditionally given to girls born on St Valentine's day.

Valentine (B)
From the Latin 'valens' meaning 'strong' or 'healthy', it was used as a first name in ancient Rome, but was made famous by St Valentine, a third-century Roman priest martyred on 14 February. (The tradition of lovers' cards is a 19th-century invention.)

Valeria (G)
Latin, meaning 'strong' or 'healthy' and the name of an important Roman family, the Valerians.

Valerie (G)
French form of Valerie, meaning 'strong' or 'healthy'. Long popular in France because it was the name of a favourite saint, it came into use in England in the early years of the 20th century.

Vanessa (G)
An 18th-century name, coined by Jonathan Swift, who wrote *Gulliver's Travels*, for his friend Esther Vanhomrigh. He took the first three letters of her surname and added Essa, a pet form of Esther. It has been a popular name since the 60s when the actress Vanessa Redgrave caught the public imagination.

Vanna (G)
Shortened form of Giovanna, the Italian form of Joan, meaning 'grace of God'.

Vashti (G)
Royal Persian name meaning 'the best'. Queen Vashti was

the wife of King Ahasuerus of Persia and she is mentioned in the Book of Esther in the Old Testament.

Vaslav (B)
Slavic form of Basil, meaning 'kingly' and the name of three eastern saints. The Russian form is Vassily.

Vaughan (B)
English form of an originally Welsh surname, meaning 'little', which is occasionally used as a Christian name.

Venetia (G)
Name of unknown origin which may have been coined by the Stanley family for an association with Venice. Venetia Stanley was a celebrated 17th-century beauty and Benjamin Disraeli wrote a popular romantic novel entitled *Venetia* (1837) which brought it into Victorian usage.

Vera (G)
A very old and popular Russian name, meaning 'faith', Vera came into use in England, along with Olga, Sonya, and Nadya, in the 1870s when there was a fashion for Russian names and has remained in more or less constant use since.

Vere (B)
Surname of the de Vére family who came over with William the Conqueror. It has occasionally been used as a Christian name since the 17th century.

Verity (G)
From Latin, meaning 'truth'. Verity was one of the 'virtue' names beloved of the Puritans.

Vernon (B)
Aristocratic Norman surname which derives from a place name in Normandy. Richard de Vernon was a companion of William the Conqueror. It became popular in the late 19th century as a result of G Meredith's character of Vernon Whitford in *The Egoist* (1879).

Veronica (G)
From Latin, meaning 'of true image' and the name given to the woman who wiped Christ's face as he walked to his crucifixion. Her name day is 4 February. Always popular on the Continent, the name reached Scotland first, when

the Earl of Kincardine married a Dutch lady called Veronica in the 17th century. It was a popular name in the 20s and 30s and later for its association with the Hollywood film star Veronica Lake.

Vesta (G)
Roman goddess of fire.

Vicky (G)
Short form of Victoria first used as a name for Princess Victoria, the Princess Royal, Queen Victoria's eldest daughter. An alternative spelling is Vicki.

Victor (B)
From Latin, meaning 'conqueror', rarely used in England until the last century when it came into use as a male form of Victoria.

Victoria (G)
From Latin, meaning 'victory'. Although popular on the Continent for many centuries, the name had never taken root in England. Alexandrina Victoria, daughter of Duke of Kent and Victoire, Dowager Princess of Leningen, changed that when she became Queen in 1837. It has become popular again in the second half of this century and now ranks in the top ten names for girls.

Victorine (G)
French form of Victor, meaning 'conqueror'.

Vida (G)
Short form of Scottish name Davida.

Vincent (B)
From Latin, meaning 'conquering'. St Vincentius was one of the three great martyr deacons put to death in Spain in the third century. Trading links with Spain in the Middle Ages brought the name into use in England although its great popularity was in the 19th century following the victory by Nelson at Cape St Vincent.

Viola (G)
Old Italian, meaning 'a violet'. An old European flower name which Chaucer and Shakespeare both used for its associations with modesty.

Violet (G)
English form of Italian Viola and French Violette. The name appeared in Scotland first, probably because of the links between the French and Scottish courts. Mary Queen of Scots had a companion called Violet Forbes. Subsequently it was a favourite Victorian name.

Violette (G)
French flower name which can be found as far back as the Middle Ages. The modern Italian form is Violetta.

Virgie (G)
Affectionate form of Virginia.

Virgil (B)
From Latin, meaning 'flourishing'.

Virginia (G)
From Latin 'virgo', meaning 'maiden'. The state of Virginia in the United States was so named in 1584 in honour of Queen Elizabeth I, the Virgin Queen, and in 1587 one of the first children born in the United States was christened Virginia.

Virginie (G)
French form of Virginia which became popular in France in the 18th century.

Vita (G)
Latin for 'life' and sometimes used as a short form of Victoria.

Vittoria (G)
Italian form of Victoria.

Vivian (B)
From Latin, 'vivus', meaning 'lively'. St Vivianus was a fifth-century saint and the name was not uncommon in the Middle Ages. It was revived at the end of the 19th century for its medieval feel.

Viviana (G)
From Latin, the feminine form of Vivian, meaning 'lively'. It often appears in the Middle Ages in the form Bibiana. Viviana has also passed into modern Italian.

Vivien (G)

Feminine form of Vivian, meaning 'lively'. Tennyson's poem 'Vivien and Merlin' popularized the name in Victorian times for its Celtic and medieval associations.

Vyvyan (B)

Welsh form of Vivian, meaning 'lively'. This originally Latin name lingered on in Celtic Britain well after the Romans had departed. There was a Celtic St Fithian of Fife in the seventh century. Oscar Wilde chose the name, at the height of the late-19th-century Celtic name revival, for his son.

W

Wallace (B)
From Anglo-Saxon meaning 'foreign'. Wallace was a Scottish family surname, Sir William Wallace being the 'hammer and scourge of England' in the 13th century. His fame was revived in the 19th century and it became a popular Christian name.

Wallis (B&G)
American form of Wallace used for both girls and boys in the United States.

Walt (B)
Shortened form of Walter which is also used as a name in its own right in the United States.

Walter (B)
From Anglo-Saxon and Old German, with associations of 'rule' and 'people', it was brought to England by the Normans. Out of fashion from the 17th century, it was revived in the 19th for its Old English feel and until the second half of the present century it was perceived as being a rather dashing name.

Wanda (G)
From Old German, meaning 'kindred'. An alternative spelling is Wenda.

Warren (B)
Surname which became a Christian name in the 19th century for its aristocratic feel. Warren Hastings was Governor General of the East India Company.

Wat (B)
Very old short form of Walter which dates from the 14th century.

Turn again, Dick Whittington

Over a third of Mayors and Lord Mayors of the City of London from 1192 to the present day were called John, William or Thomas, John being the most favoured name with 134 appearances over 800 years.

John	124 times
William	89 "
Thomas	72 "
Robert	32 "
Richard	30 "
George	22 "
James	21 "
Henry	18 "
Charles	14 "
Nicholas	12 "
Edward	10 "
David	5 "

Eighteenth-century Lord Mayors were the most imaginatively named. Micajah, Crisp, Brass, Brook, Brackley, Marshe, Watkins, Slingsby, Barlow and Harvey make up a tenth of their list. Meanwhile a Bracewell, Denys, Noel, Cuthbert, Cullum, Murray and Greville have added colour in the second half of the 20th century – and a single Mary, Dame Mary Donaldson who held office in 1983, the first and only female Lord Mayor of the City of London.

Wayne (B)
Surname which became a Christian name in the 50s for its association with John Wayne.

Wendy (G)
Created by J M Barrie for *Peter Pan* stories. The small daughter of friends of his called him 'fwendy', meaning

friend. After a while it became fwendy-wendy and from this the inspiration for Wendy Darling was born. It was a popular name in the 50s.

Wesley (B)
Surname which came to be used as a Christian name among nonconformists for its association with the churchman John Wesley.

Whitney (G)
American surname of English origin made famous by Josiah Dwight Whitney (1819–96) who had one of the highest peaks in the Rockies named after him.

Wilbur (B)
From Dutch surname Wildeboer which was taken to the United States in the early 19th century. It became common as a Christian name after the aviation successes of Wilbur and Orville Wright.

Wilf (B)
Short form of Wilfred or Wilfrid.

Wilfrid (B)
Old English, with associations of 'will' and 'peace'. St Wilfrith, or Wilfrid, was Bishop of York in the seventh century and his name remained popular in the area for many centuries. It was revived at the end of the 19th century as a venerable saint's name.

Wilhelmina (G)
Feminine form of Wilhelm, the German version of William, which became popular under the Hanoverian kings in the 18th century. Oliver Goldsmith who wrote *The Vicar of Wakefield* called one of his characters Carolina Wilhelmina Amelia Skeggs.

Wilkie (B)
Also written Wilkey. Originally a short form of Wilkin.

Will (B)
Short form of William which dates from the Middle Ages. William Shakespeare was known to his friends as Will.

William (B)
Despite its Old German origin and the associated meaning of 'will' and 'helmet', William has for centuries been a quintessentially English name. It was the most popular christening name for boys in the early Middle Ages, and from the 16th to the 19th centuries one in five boys was called William. Bill came from Old English Bil.

Willie (B)
Scottish short form of William.

Willow (G)
English, the name first appeared in the 60s.

Wilma (G)
Shortened form of Wilhelmina.

Wilmot (B)
Late medieval form of William which has been in occasional use.

Winifred (G)
Old English, meaning 'blessed reconciliation'. St Winifred, or St Gwenfrewi, was a Welsh saint whose well was thought to be miraculous. Her saint's day is 3 November and her name was a favourite with the Victorians.

Winona (G)
North American Indian Sioux, meaning 'first born daughter'; it can also be spelt Wenonah. The name appears in Longfellow's epic poem 'Hiawatha' (1855).

Winston (B)
Surname of the Winston family of Standish in Gloucestershire. Sarah Winston married John, Duke of Marlborough and called her son, who was born in 1620, Winston Churchill. It was his descendant who became the great Prime Minister and saw the name being taken up for patriotic reasons. The Dutch, also, chose it as a name for babies born during the German Occupation.

Wynn (B)
Welsh, meaning 'fair'. The Celts often gave names that reflected colouring or complexion.

X

Xanthe (G)
Greek, meaning 'yellow'. It is pronounced Zan-thee.

Xavier (B)
Basque place name. St Francis Xavier, the early Jesuit priest who travelled to India, took his name from the place of his birth, the Castle of Xavier in the Basque country.

Y

Yasmin (G)
From Persian, meaning 'jasmine flower'. An ancient Arabic and Persian name it appeared in England in 1922 following the publication of James Elroy Flecker's poetic Eastern play, *Hassan*. In France the name is written Yasmine.

Yehudi (B)
From Hebrew, meaning 'praise'.

Yolanda (G)
Old French form of Italian Viola, meaning 'violet'.

Yuri (B)
Russian form of George, meaning 'tiller of the ground'.

Yves (B)
Ancient Breton name meaning 'lord' which was originally spelt Ives and is related to the Welsh name Ifor. One of Charlemagne's knights was called Yves. It is one of the classic French names.

Yvette (G)
French feminine form of Yves, meaning 'little Yves'.

Yvonne (G)
Oldest French feminine form of Yves. It was a popular name in the United States in the 30s and 40s.

Z

Zachariah (B)
Hebrew, meaning 'the Lord is renowned'. It appears in the Old Testament as the name of a king of Israel and a prophet. The favoured English version was Zachary.

Zara (G)
Arabic, meaning 'splendour of the dawn'. It was the name of the African queen in Congreve's *The Mourning Bride* (1697).

Zenobia (G)
From Greek, meaning 'life from Zeus'. Zenobia was the Queen of Palmyra.

Zoe (G)
Greek, meaning 'life', the name used for the Hebrew 'Euba' or 'Eve'. Zoe became a popular Christian name in the Eastern Roman Empire, used by royalty and commoners alike, but did not appear in England until the mid-19th century. Since the late 50s it has been a common Christian name.

Zuleika (G)
Persian name, meaning 'brilliant beauty'. Zuleika was the heroine of Byron's *The Bride of Abydos* and Max Beerbohm's fanciful novel *Zuleika Dobson*. The Sanskrit form, meaning 'beautiful', is Zulekha.

Appendix

Boys

One syllable

Art	Gwyn	Nye	Aidan
Bart	Hal	Paul	Alain
Bede	Hank	Piers	Alan
Bjorn	Hans	Ralph	Allan
Blake	Hu	Raoul	Aldous
Blase	Hugh	Ray	Alon
Bram	Huw	Rex	Alvin
Bruce	Ike	Rick	Alvis
Burt	Jack	Rob	Alwyn
Carl	Jacques	Rolf	Ambrose
Chad	Jake	Rolph	Amos
Clark	James	Ross	André
Claud	Jay	Roy	Andrew
Claude	Jem	Sam	Angus
Clem	Jock	Saul	Anton
Clive	Joel	Scott	Arnold
Craig	John	Sean	Arthur
Dai	Joos	Seth	Asa
Dale	Juan	Serge	Ashley
Dean	Jude	Shaun	Aubrey
Dick	Jules	Steen	Austin
Dirk	Karl	Tam	Axel
Doyle	Keith	Teague	Banquo
Duff	Kim	Ted	Bartley
Dwayne	Kit	Vaughan	Basil
Dwight	Kyle	Vere	Bearach
Finn	Lance	Walt	Bernard
Flann	Lee	Wat	Bertie
Floyd	Leigh	Wayne	Bertram
Frank	Lloyd	Wilf	Bevis
George	Luke	Will	Boris
Giles	Marc	Wynn	Bradley
Glen	Mark	Yves	Brendam
Glenn	Max		Brian
Glyn	Nat		Bruno
Grant	Neal	*Two syllables*	Bryan
Guy	Ned	Aaron	Byron
	Neil	Abel	Callum
	Nial	Adair	Carey
	Nils	Adam	Carolo

Caspar	Dunstan	Gawen	Irwin
Castor	Dylan	Geoffrey	Isaac
Cecil	Eamon	Geordie	Isaak
Cedric	Eben	Geraint	Ivan
Charlie	Edgar	Gerald	Ivo
Charley	Edmond	Gerard	Ivor
Chensay	Edmund	Germaine	Jacob
Clarence	Edward	Gerry	Jamie
Clayton	Edwin	Gervase	Jason
Clemnet	Edwy	Gilbert	Jasper
Clifford	Eli	Gilroy	Jerome
Clovis	Ellis	Godfrey	Jerry
Colon	Eldred	Gordon	Jervis
Colin	Elton	Graeme	Jesse
Colum	Elvis	Graham	Jesus
Conal	Emlyn	Griffith	Jethro
Conan	Enoch	Haldane	Jordan
Conor	Eric	Hamon	Joseph
Corin	Erik	Hamisth	Justin
Cory	Ernest	Hanno	Kegan
Courtney	Errol	Harald	Kelvin
Crispin	Erskine	Hardy	Kenelm
Curran	Erwin	Harold	Kenneth
Curtis	Esme	Haroun	Kerry
Cyril	Esmond	Harry	Kevin
Cyrus	Euan	Harvey	Kieran
Damon	Eugene	Hassan	Knud
Darcy	Eustace	Hayden	Lachlan
Darrell	Evan	Hector	Larry
Darren	Evelyn	Helmut	Laurence
David	Ewan	Henry	Lawrence
Denis	Ezra	Herbert	Leo
Dennis	Farquhar	Herman	Leon
Denys	Feargus	Hiram	Leonard
Densil	Felix	Homer	Leroy
Derick	Fergal	Horace	Leslie
Deryck	Fergus	Howard	Lester
Dermot	Fidel	Howell	Lewis
Desmond	Fingal	Hubert	Liam
Dewi	Fitzroy	Hugo	Lindsay
Dexter	Fletcher	Humfrey	Lorin
Diarmuit	Foster	Hywel	Louis
Dickon	Francis	Iain	Lucas
Digby	Franklin	Ian	Madoc
Donal	Fraser	Idris	Magnus
Donald	Gareth	Ievan	Malcolm
Dougal	Garfield	Ifan	Malise
Douglas	Gary	Ifor	Manfred
Dudley	Gaston	Ira	Manley
Duncan	Gavin	Irving	Marcel

Marco	Pedro	Stirling	Anerin
Marcus	Penrose	St John	Anthony
Marshal	Penwyn	St George	Antony
Martin	Pepe	Stuart	Archibald
Martyn	Percy	Talbot	Ariel
Marvin	Perry	Tancred	Auberon
Matthew	Peter	Terence	Augustus
Maurice	Philip	Theo	Balthasar
Merlin	Pierre	Thomas	Barnabas
Mervin	Quentin	Thurston	Barnaby
Michael	Quincy	Titus	Benedick
Michel	Rabbie	Toby	Benedict
Moses	Rabi	Tony	Benjamin
Mungo	Ramsey	Torquil	Bernardo
Munro	Ranald	Trefor	Casimir
Murray	Randal	Trevor	Charlemagne
Nathan	Randolph	Tristan	Christian
Nelson	Ranulf	Tristram	Christopher
Nestor	Raymond	Tudor	Columbus
Neville	Reuben	Tybalt	Constantine
Niall	Rhodri	Tyrone	Cosimo
Nico	Richard	Uwen	Damian
Nigel	Robert	Vaslav	Darius
Noah	Robin	Vernon	Doggory
Noel	Rodney	Victor	Dominic
Norman	Roger	Vincent	Donovan
Nowell	Roland	Virgil	Dorian
Ogden	Ronald	Wallace	Elias
Olaf	Rory	Wallis	Emanuel
Oleg	Rowan	Walter	Erasmus
Omar	Rowland	Warren	Ferdinand
Oran	Royston	Wesley	Flavian
Orson	Rudolf	Wilbur	Francesco
Osbert	Rudyard	Wilfrid	Frédéric
Osborn	Rufus	Wilkie	Frederick
Oscar	Rupert	Willie	Gyodor
Osmond	Russell	Wilmot	Gabriel
Oswald	Ryan	Winston	Hannibal
Osric	Sacha	Yuri	Hilary
Oswin	Samson		Horatio
Otto	Sandro	*Three syllables*	Immanuel
Otis	Selwyn	Abraham	Inigo
Owain	Sidney	Adamnan	Isambard
Owen	Sigmund	Adrian	Jeremy
Pablo	Simon	Aeneas	Jolyon
Pádraic	Stanley	Alasdair	Jonathan
Padrig	Stefan	Alexis	Joscelyn
Pasco	Stephen	Algernon	Joshua
Patrick	Steven	Anatole	Josiah
Pavel	Stewart	Andreas	Julian

Leopold
Lionel
Lucian
Ludovic
Lysander
Malachy
Marius
Marmaduke
Montague
Mortimer
Nicholas
Ninian
Oberon
Oliver
Oriel
Orlando
Perceval
Peregrine
Phineas
Reginald
Saladin
Saloman
Salvator
Samuel
Soloman
Thaddeus
Theobald
Theodore
Timothy
Tobias
Trelawney
Ulysses
Valentine
Vivian
Vyvyan
William
Xavier
Yehudi

Four syllables
Aleksandr
Alexander
Alisander
Amadeus
Baldasarre
Bartholomew
Cornelius
Giacomo
Lodovico
Napoleon

Nathaniel
Sebastian
Silvester
Zachariah

Five syllables
Maximilian

Girls

One syllable
Ann
Anne
Babs
Bea
Bess
Beth
Ceit
Claire
Clare
Claude
Em
Eve
Faine
Faith
Fay
Fleur
Flore
Gail
Gay
Gayle
Gill
Grace
Gwen
Hope
Jane
Jayne
Jean
Jeanne
Jill
Joan
Joy
June
Kate
Kay
Lark
Lee
Lyn
Lynn

Lys
Madge
Mae
Maeve
Maude
May
Meg
Merle
Miles
Nan
Niahm
Noor
Raine
Rose
Ruth
Sîan
Storm

Two syllables
Ada
Adah
Adele
Agnes
Aileen
Ailsa
Alice
Aline
Alix
Alma
Alys
Amber
Amy
Andrée
Anis
Anna
Annette
Annie
Anwen
Aphra
April
Arleen
Ashley
Astra
Astrid
Audrey
Ava
Averil
Avril
Babette
Beatrice

Beatrix
Becky
Bella
Bernice
Bertha
Beryl
Bethan
Betty
Beulah
Biddy
Blanca
Blodwen
Blossom
Bonnie
Branwen
Brenda
Bridget
Bridie
Bridgid
Brigitte
Bronwen
Bronya
Candace
Cara
Carey
Carla
Carmen
Carole
Carys
Caitlin
Catharine
Catherine
Catrin
Celeste
Ceris
Charlotte
Charmaine
Chelsea
Cherry
Cheryl
Chloë
Christine
Chrystal
Cilla
Cindy
Claudette
Claudine
Clea
Cleo
Clio

Clodagh	Emma	Hayley	Kelly
Cluny	Ena	Hazel	Keren
Colette	Enid	Heather	Kerry
Colleen	Eppie	Hebe	Kirsty
Constance	Esha	Hedda	Kitty
Cara	Esmé	Heddwen	Kylie
Coral	Estelle	Hedy	Lalla
Courtney	Esther	Heidi	Lana
Crystal	Ethel	Helen	Lauren
Cuthbert	Etta	Helga	Leah
Dagmar	Evan	Hester	Leeanne
Daisy	Evelym	Hilda	Leila
Dana	Fanny	Holly	Lena
Daphne	Felice	Honor	Lesley
Darcy	Fifi	Ida	Lettice
Debra	Flora	Ilse	Letty
Deirdre	Florence	Imma	Lexy
Delphine	Florie	Ines	Liane
Denise	Franca	Inge	Libby
Diane	Frances	Ingrid	Lilac
Dickon	Francine	Iris	Lily
Dido	Francoise	Irma	Linda
Dilys	Freda	Iseult	Lindsay
Dinah	Freya	Ishbel	Lisa
Dianne	Gaia	Ismay	Lizzy
Dodie	Geena	Isla	Lois
Dolly	Gemma	Isolde	Lola
Donna	Georgette	Ivey	Lora
Dora	Georgia	Jana	Lorna
Doreen	Gerda	Jancis	Lorraine
Doris	Germaine	Janet	Louise
Drina	Gertrude	Janice	Loulou
Dulce	Ghislaine	Janine	Lucette
Dulcie	Gigi	Jasmine	Lucille
Eartha	Gina	Jeanette	Lucy
Edith	Ginny	Jessie	Lulu
Edna	Gladys	Joanne	Lynette
Effie	Glenda	Josie	Lysanne
Eibhlín	Glenys	Josette	Mabel
Eileen	Glynis	Judith	Maddy
Eirene	Graínne	Julie	Madlin
Elain	Greta	Justine	Mada
Elaine	Gretchen	Karen	Maggie
Elise	Gwenan	Kasia	Maidie
Ella	Gwenda	Katharine	Máire
Ellen	Gwyneth	Katherine	Máirin
Ellie	Hadwen	Kathleen	Maisie
Elsa	Haidee	Katie	Manon
Elspeth	Hannah	Katya	Margot
Elwyn	Hayden	Kayleigh	Mari

Marie	Patience	Sheryl	Willow
Marta	Paula	Shirley	Wilma
Martha	Paulette	Sibyl	Xanthe
Mary	Pauline	Sigrid	Yasmin
Maureen	Peggy	Sile	Yasmine
Mavis	Peta	Simone	Yvette
Maxine	Petra	Sinéad	Yvonne
Megan	Phoeve	Siobhán	Zara
Menna	Phyllis	Solange	Zelda
Meraud	Pia	Sonia	Zeinab
Meryl	Pippa	Sonya	Zoe
Meta	Polly	Sophie	
Mhairi	Poppy	Sorcha	*Three syllables*
Mia	Portia	Stacey	Abigail
Michèle	Prudence	Stella	Adela
Michelle	Psyche	Sukey	Adelaide
Mildred	Queenie	Susan	Adina
Mimi	Rabi	Suzanne	Adrienne
Minette	Rachel	Sylvie	Agatha
Moira	Rhea	Tacey	Agneta
Molly	Rhoda	Tamar	Alana
Mona	Rhona	Tamsin	Alberta
Mora	Rita	Tania	Alethea
Morag	Romaine	Tansy	Alison
Morgan	Romy	Tara	Allegra
Morna	Rosa	Tegan	Alethea
Myra	Rosanne	Tessa	Alison
Myrna	Rozanne	Thea	Allegra
Myrtle	Ruby	Thecla	Althea
Nadine	Ruthie	Thelma	Amanda
Nancy	Sabre	Thora	Aminta
Nerys	Sadie	Tilda	Anais
Nesta	Saffron	Tina	Andrea
Neva	Sally	Topaz	Andrina
Nicole	Sancha	Tracy	Angela
Nina	Sandra	Ulla	Aneira
Noelle	Sapphire	Una	Anita
Nora	Sara	Unna	Annabel
Norah	Sarah	Vanna	Annika
Noreen	Scarlett	Vashti	Annona
Norma	Selma	Vera	Anthea
Odette	Senga	Vesta	Antoinette
Olga	Seumas	Vicky	Ariel
Olive	Shannon	Vida	Artemis
Olwen	Shari	Virgie	Athena
Ondine	Sharon	Vita	Augusta
Oona	Shelagh	Wallis	Aurora
Oonagh	Sheila	Wanda	Aveline
Opal	Shelley	Wendy	Ayesha
Orsa	Sheena	Whitney	Barbara

Barbary	Demelza	Harriet	Letitia
Bathsheba	Diana	Helena	Lewanna
Belinda	Dolores	Heloise	Lilibet
Benita	Dominique	Hepzibar	Lilian
Berenice	Dorinda	Hereward	Livia
Bernadette	Dorothy	Hermia	Loretta
Bettina	Drusilla	Hermione	Louisa
Bianca	Dulcia	Hilary	Lucasta
Bonita	Ebony	Hildegarde	Lucia
Brigitta	Edwina	Honesty	Lucilla
Brittany	Eiluned	Horatia	Lucinda
Brunilla	Eleanor	Ianthe	Lucretia
Bryony	Electra	Idina	Ludmilla
Calypso	Elena	Iduna	Luisa
Candida	Eldreda	Ilona	Lydia
Candia	Elinor	Imogen	Madeleine
Caroline	Eliza	India	Magdalen
Carolyn	Elissa	Iona	Malati
Cassandra	Eloise	Irene	Marcella
Catriona	Elvira	Isabeau	Marcia
Cecilia	Emelie	Isabel	Margaret
Cecily	Emerald	Isabelle	Margery
Celia	Emily	Isobel	Marjorie
Celina	Emmeline	Ivana	Marguerite
Ceridwen	Erasma	Jacquetta	Maria
Charity	Erica	Janetta	Marianne
Christabel	Erinna	Jermima	Mariel
Christian	Ernestine	Jennifer	Mariette
Cicely	Estrella	Jessica	Marigold
Claribel	Eugenie	Joanna	Marilyn
Clarinda	Evelina	Jocasta	Marina
Clarissa	Favia	Jocunda	Marion
Claudia	Fedora	Johanna	Marleen
Clemency	Fenella	Joscelyn	Martina
Clementine	Fernanda	Josepha	Mary-Anne
Cleone	Finola	Josephine	Mathilda
Clothilda	Fiona	Juanita	Melanie
Constancy	Fionngula	Julia	Melina
Coralie	Flavia	Juliet	Melissa
Corinna	Francesca	Katinka	Melitta
Cosima	Genevieve	Kerensa	Melody
Cressida	Georgina	Keturah	Mercedes
Cynthia	Gilberta	Keziah	Meredith
Dahlia	Gilbertine	Kimberley	Meriel
Daria	Gillina	Lalita	Merrilyn
Davida	Gloria	Lamorna	Michaela
Deanna	Grania	Larissa	Millicent
Deborah	Griselda	Lavender	Mirabel
Delia	Gwendolen	Lavinia	Miranda
Delilah	Gwenonwy	Leonie	Miriam

Modesty	Rosamund	Violet	Genovefa
Minoca	Rosanna	Violette	Georgiana
Morwenna	Rosemary	Virginie	Henrietta
Muriel	Rowena	Vivien	Ileana
Myfanwy	Rufina	Winona	Isabella
Nadia	Sabina	Winifred	Isadora
Natalie	Sabrina	Yolanda	Jacqueline
Natasha	Salome	Zamira	January
Nerina	Samantha	Zuleika	Juliana
Merissa	Sapphira		Katerina
Nicola	Saranna	*Four syllables*	Leonora
Nigella	Saskia	Alexandra	Margareta
Nuala	Selena	Ambrosia	Margherita
Ottilie	Serena	Angelica	Melesina
Ottoline	Sibella	Angelina	Mélusine
Paloma	Sidonie	Antonia	Natalia
Pamela	Silvana	Arabella	Natalina
Pandora	Sophia	Araminta	Octavia
Patricia	Speranza	Ariadne	Olivia
Peony	Stephanie	Atalanta	Olympia
Perdita	Susanna	Basilia	Orphelia
Petula	Susannah	Benedicta	Penelope
Philippa	Sylvia	Bernardina	Persephone
Phyllida	Tabitha	Caterine	Petronella
Poppea	Tallulah	Constantia	Philomena
Priscilla	Tamara	Cordelia	Seraphina
Prunella	Teresa	Daniella	Tatiana
Ramona	Theresa	Dorabella	Theodora
Rebecca	Tiffany	Dorothea	Thomasina
Regina	Tresilla	Eleanora	Titania
Renata	Trixe	Elisabeth	Valeria
Rhiannon	Ulrica	Elisheba	Victoria
Richenda	Unity	Elizabeth	Vittoria
Roberta	Ursula	Emmanuelle	Viviana
Robina	Valerie	Ethelia	Wilhelmina
Roderick	Vanessa	Evangeline	
Romola	Venetia	Felicia	*Five syllables*
Rosaleen	Verity	Felicity	Alexandrina
Rosalie	Victorine	Fiammetta	Anastasia
Rosalind	Viola	Frederika	Artemisia